Exploring The Road

BASED ON M. SCOTT PECK'S CLASSIC BEST SELLER
THE ROAD LESS TRAVELED
A New Psychology of Love,
Traditional Values and Spiritual Growth

A STUDY GUIDE FOR SMALL GROUPS
A WORKBOOK FOR INDIVIDUALS
A STEP-BY-STEP GUIDE FOR GROUP LEADERS

Less Traveled

by
Alice and Walden Howard

With a foreword by M. Scott Peck, M.D.

SIMON AND SCHUSTER
New York

Published by Simon and Schuster
A Division of Simon & Schuster, Inc.
Simon & Schuster Building
Rockefeller Center
1230 Avenue of the Americas
New York, New York 10020

SIMON AND SCHUSTER and colophon are registered trademarks of
Simon & Schuster, Inc.

Designed by Irving Perkins Associates
Manufactured in the United States of America

1 2 3 4 5 6 7 8 9 10

Library of Congress Cataloging in Publication Data

Howard, Alice, date.
Exploring The road less traveled.

"Based on M. Scott Peck's . . . The road less traveled."
1. Peck, M. Scott (Morgan Scott), 1936–   . The road less traveled—
Problems, exercises, etc.   2. Maturation (Psychology)—Problems, exercises, etc.
3. Psychology and religion—Problems, exercises, etc.   I. Howard, Walden.
II. Peck, M. Scott (Morgan Scott), 1936–Road less traveled.   III. Title.
BF710.H69   1985   158'.1   85-1819

ISBN: 0-671-54292-3

The authors gratefully acknowledge permission to reprint excerpts from the following:

Christian Life Patterns, by Evelyn Eaton Whitehead and James D. Whitehead; pp. 6–8. Copyright © 1979 by Evelyn Eaton Whitehead and James D. Whitehead. Reprinted by permission of Doubleday & Co., Inc.

Excerpt from an unpublished sermon by

(continued on page 187)

Contents

Foreword

In writing to me, one of the initial admirers of *The Road Less Traveled* said, "It's not really your book, you know." She was, of course, correct. I do not think that I can take much credit for it. *The Road Less Traveled* is a better book than I could have written. It was a gift to me and through me to all my fellow pilgrims.

Now Walden and Alice Howard have written this self-study guide for small groups so as to further enhance the gift. And it is a gift in its own right. I well know the care and thoughtfulness with which it has been prepared. It has my wholehearted blessing. I presume to suspect that it also has God's blessing. For above all else, the divine intent is that we travel Godward.

M. Scott Peck
New Preston, Connecticut

An Invitation

If life is a journey, the choice of roads we take is crucial. Scott Peck invites us to travel toward spiritual growth. And we invite you to join with others in a process that will support and encourage you on the way.

The Road Less Traveled charts a new course for many of us contemporary Americans who are searching for ways to deal with the problems of everyday life. In the midst of dozens of conflicting voices vying for our attention and promising us simple solutions to our problems, we hear the realistic words of Scott Peck saying, "Life is difficult," and an inner voice says, "He's right. Life *is* difficult, and there's no dodging its challenges." For herein lies the road to reality and integrity.

If you have read the book and pondered over its ideas, you probably have wanted to discuss them with others and, beyond that, to experiment with adopting them into your framework of behavior. But most of us need help in knowing how to apply new concepts to our lives.

Most of us learn best, *really* learn, from our own experience— not simply from having things happen to us but from reflecting on what happens, both alone and in exchanges with others, so that the meaning of our experience becomes clear and we can make choices based on growing awareness rather than unchallenged assumptions.

We learn best by doing, not so much from hearing or seeing, but acting in some way that puts us in touch with where we are and where we want to be. This is no new discovery. Confucius said, centuries ago,

> I hear and I forget;
> I see and I remember;
> I do and I understand.

As one educator has put it, "Everything we do involves some kind of learning. Reflecting on the past, acting in the present, planning for the future, all clearly suggest the fundamental process of learning by doing."*

Very often such learning is enhanced and deepened when we work with a supportive group—a group where others are wrestling with the same questions we are, where we can do more than discuss ideas objectively. We need a chance to work experimentally with the ideas, as scientists experiment in a laboratory, and then apply our findings to our lives.

What follows in this book is a study and discussion manual that grew out of a 12-session course first held in our church in Colum-

* John D. Ingalls, *A Trainer's Guide to Andragogy* (Washington, D.C./:U.S. Department of Health, Education and Welfare, 1972), p. 3.

10

bia, Maryland, in the winter of 1981. Twenty of us met each Sunday evening for two hours, reading ahead in the book in preparation for the coming session while four of us met in advance to assimilate the material and prepare experiential exercises that would connect it to our individual lives.

From our group process came these guidelines for your study that have been tested in dozens of other groups since. We are happy that all across our country women and men like you are using Scott Peck's thoughtful and insightful book as a guide for their life journey. We trust you will find this study process helpful as you pursue it with a few other likeminded individuals.

How to Use This Guide

This guide has been designed for use in group discussion meetings, although it is easily adaptable for those of you who may wish to use it for individual study and reflection, or for informal discussion with a friend and fellow reader.

COMMITMENT As you begin, ask yourself how serious you are about working with ideas and personal challenges in a group session. Are you willing to venture in sharing some of your feelings and experiences? Will you give priority to preparation, attendance and participation? It will be an exciting process, worth all the effort you put into it.

TIME We found two-hour sessions to be most valuable and recommend that time frame, though we suspect that some groups may be forced to work within narrower time constrictions. But whatever time is agreed upon, will you commit yourself to regular and prompt attendance? Sessions should start and end on time and you should report to your group leader before the meeting if you will not be able to attend.

CHECKING IN Time will usually be provided in the opening minutes of each group session to reflect on what has gone on in the time that has elapsed between sessions—to think about what you have learned or situations that have occurred that affect your ability to focus on the group's new agenda. You need to be sure you are "present" mentally and emotionally as well as physically in order to benefit from each session.

GUIDELINES Instructions for each exercise will be quite explicit, but keep in mind these important *guidelines:* (a) Avoid merely theorizing or speaking abstractly about your philosophy of life; speak rather out of your personal experience ("This is how I've experienced that," or "This is how that works for me," for example). (b) Use "I" statements, rather than statements like "One finds that . . ." or "You find that . . ." Simply say, "I think . . ." or "I find that . . ." (c) Be specific; keep it brief but tell what, when and where when you relate an experience. (d) Allow your thoughts, feelings and reflections to flow. Don't edit yourself or sit in judgment on yourself. (e) Finally, it is imperative that everyone respect confidentiality in the group, so that nothing of a personal nature is reported outside the group.

LEADERSHIP The role of your group leader (or leaders) does not require that they be experts, but that they facilitate the learning process in the group. Hopefully, they will enter as fully as possible into the process, sharing in the exercises with you as they are able. Their modeling from time to time, out of their own experience, should encourage your honesty and sharing of personal insights.

Their participation will also help them test the effectiveness of each exercise and assist the progress of the group in understanding the issues being dealt with.

GOING ON You will find supplementary readings under the heading, *Resources for the Road.* In addition, you may have favorite passages that bear on the subject you are studying that you may wish to share with the group.

We recommend that you acquire a notebook that can serve as a record of the journey you are about to undertake and that will give you additional pages on which to note your thoughts and feelings. Time will often be given in your group sessions for writing in this notebook, so be sure to bring it to each session along with your copy of *The Road Less Traveled* and this study guide.

This book consists of two sections. At the back are guidelines for the group leader which it is not necessary for you to read. In fact, the sessions will be more helpful for you if you do not try to anticipate what is coming but concentrate instead on reading the assigned pages in *The Road Less Traveled* and do the suggested exercises.

PREPARATION The material that follows assumes that you will meet in twelve group sessions, although your group leader may choose to combine or expand this number. Note, however, that we have included only eleven lessons, to be used *after* the first eleven group sessions, each with space in which to reflect back on what happened to you in the session just completed and several questions designed to sharpen your focus on the material to be covered in the next session. The more thoroughly you prepare the more benefit will come to you in the sessions themselves.

> MY COMMITMENT
>
> I will take time to prepare myself for each session.
> I will take responsibility for what I need to learn.
> I will avoid speaking in broad generalizations.
> I will share my true feelings and concerns.
> When I share I will be succinct and to the point.
> I will respect confidentiality outside the group.

Delaying Gratification

Looking Back

In the first session of your group you spent a few minutes getting acquainted with your leader(s) and the other participants as well as getting an overview of the course and the guidelines by which your group will function.

You discussed the basic assumptions that underlie Scott Peck's writing: that *life is difficult*, and that it is so because it is "a series of problems" that we often avoid because "the process of confronting and solving problems is a painful one. . . . Yet it is in this whole process of meeting and solving problems that life has its meaning." You shared among yourselves some of the ways in which you typically avoid problems and reflected on a specific situation that you finally confronted and from which you learned and grew.

What happened *to you* in the session, and how do you feel as a result? Take a few minutes to record your feelings, your observations, your insights and unresolved issues.

_____

_____

_____

_____

_____

_____

_____

_____

_____

_____

_____

What types of problems are hardest for you to deal with?_____

_____

_____

How willing are you to confront these problems in order to change and grow?_____

_____

_____

You may wish to share some of this as your group begins its next session.

18

Looking Ahead

READING ASSIGNMENT: Read pages 1–32 in *The Road Less Traveled*, paying special attention to pages 18–20, which describe the first tool for solving problems: "Delaying Gratification." Only after you have read the assignment, do the following exercises in preparation for your next group session.

Childhood Messages

1. To what degree were your basic needs met as a child? (Let 0 represent "unmet" and 10 "fully met.")

	0	1	2	3	4	5	6	7	8	9	10
Your own space and possessions											
Your right to privacy											
A dependable schedule											
Someone who listened to you											
Affirmation of your worth											
Freedom to make choices											
Affection shown to you											
Promises made to you and kept											

2. Who was there for you when you came home? _____

_____

_____

3. How secure did you feel in your world? _____

_____

_____

4. What messages did you receive about delaying gratification?

_____

_____

5. What gratifications were you denied, and why? _____

_____

Cultural Forces

6. What forces in the world today encourage or discourage delaying gratification? List as many as you can think of:

ENCOURAGE DELAY Need for education (for example)	DISCOURAGE DELAY Easy access to credit cards (for example)
_____	_____
_____	_____
_____	_____
_____	_____
_____	_____
_____	_____

7. Which forces have the most power in your life? Underline them. Then write how these forces impact on your life:

_____

_____

_____

_____

_____

_____

_____

Resources for the Road

It takes so much to be a full human being that there are very few who have the enlightenment or the courage to pay the price.

One has to abandon altogether the search for security and reach out to the risk of living with both arms. One has to embrace the world like a lover, and yet demand no easy return of love.

One has to accept pain as a condition of existence. One has to court doubt and darkness as the cost of existence. One needs a will stubborn in conflict, but apt always to the total acceptance of living and dying.

Morris L. West,
The Shoes of the Fisherman

Every one of us gladly turns away from his problems; if possible, they must not be mentioned, or, better still, their exis-

21

tence is denied. We wish to make our lives simple, certain, and smooth, and for that reason problems are taboo. We want to have certainties and no doubts—results and no experiments—without even seeing that certainties can arise only through doubt and results only through experiment. The artful denial of a problem will not produce conviction; on the contrary, a wider and higher consciousness is required to give us the certainty and clarity we need.

C. G. JUNG,
Collected Works, Vol. 8

Problems exist because we exist and mostly because we exist in relationship with each other. Reactions are always a part of the problem because it is in and through them that we experience the sadness, pain, and tension that subjectively define a problem for us. Our reactions are part of the problem, but, as we understand and integrate them, they become part of the solution.

EUGENE KENNEDY,
Living with Everyday Problems

Man has places in his heart which do not yet exist, and into them he enters suffering in order that they may have existence.

LEON BLOY

In his recent book, *New Rules: Searching for Self-fulfillment in a World Turned Upside Down* (Random House: 1981), the noted social researcher, Daniel Yankelovich, describes the narcissistic "me first" attitude that became pervasive in America in our recent past: "In the place of the self-denial ethic that once ruled American life, we now find people who refuse to deny themselves *anything* . . . on the strange moral principle that 'I have a duty to myself.' "

But Yankelovich notes hopeful signs that a cultural revolution is beginning to take place. "In dwelling on their own needs," he reports, many Americans "discover that the inner journey brings loneliness and depression." The ethic of the seventies is giving way to "a new ethic of commitment . . . a longing for connectedness, commitment and creative expression."

The book, which draws heavily on case histories of young Americans whom Yankelovich documents, is an important one and we highly recommend its reading.

In the Jewish and Christian Scriptures (as in many others, no doubt) much is made of *waiting* and of *patience*. Consider the forty years the Israelites had to spend in the wilderness after their deliverance from Egypt and before being allowed to enter the Promised Land.

"Remember," Moses said to them, "how the Lord your God led you all the way in the desert these forty years, to humble you and to test you in order to know what was in your heart, whether or not you would keep his commands. He humbled you, causing you to hunger, to teach you that man does not live on bread alone but on every word that comes from the mouth of the Lord" (Deuteronomy 8:2,3).

Some wants are more important than others. Some gratification is only temporary, while some is long-term and lasting. Jesus quoted Moses' very words in the time of tremendous testing in the wilderness that prepared him for his public ministry. (See Matthew 4:4.) And he demonstrated his priorities to his disciples when he said, "I have food to eat that you know nothing of" (John 4:32).

Many of the psalms speak of waiting:

Be still before the Lord and wait patiently for him;
Do not fret when men succeed in their ways,
  when they carry out their wicked schemes. . . .
Do not fret—it leads only to evil. . . .
But those who hope in the Lord will inherit the land.

PSALM 37:7–9

In the New Testament there is much counsel for patient waiting to receive what is best for us. Hebrews 11:1–40 is a long recital of those who, in Israel's history, persevered although they did not all receive the reward they hoped for. There follows this urging to the followers of Jesus: "Therefore . . . let us run with perseverance the race marked out for us. Let us fix our eyes on Jesus, the author and perfecter of our faith, who for the joy set before him, endured the cross, scorning its shame" (Hebrews 12:1,2).

This same theme appears in the Letter of James, "Consider it pure joy, my brothers," he says, "whenever you face trials of many kinds, because you know that the testing of your faith develops perseverance. Perseverance must finish its work so that you may be mature and complete, not lacking anything" (James 1:2,4).

And Peter describes the same pattern of life: trials and difficulty may be your lot now, but reward will surely come. "Now for a little while you may have had to suffer grief in all kinds of trials. These have come so that your faith—of greater worth than gold, which perishes . . . may be proved genuine and may result in praise, glory, and honor when Jesus Christ is revealed" (I Peter 1:6,7).

St. Augustine, centuries later, voiced what was for him the supreme gratification, when he prayed, "O Lord, Thou has made us for Thyself and our hearts are restless until they find their rest in Thee."

24

What do you want most in life and what are you prepared to sacrifice to attain it?_____

_____

_____

_____

LESSON TWO
Accepting Responsibility

Looking Back

In your second session you may have experienced receiving and delaying gratification in a playful exercise of "shoulder tapping." You recalled childhood messages and present cultural forces that encourage or discourage delay.

What happened *to you* in the session? What interactions or insights do you want to record? What issues remain unresolved?

_____

_____

_____

_____

_____

_____

_____

_____

_____

_____

_____

_____

What issue of satisfying or delaying gratification are you struggling with this week?_____

_____

_____

_____

Looking Ahead

READING ASSIGNMENT: Read pages 32–44 in *The Road Less Traveled* and review pages 15–18, especially recalling Peck's words: "Life is a series of problems. Do we want to moan about them or solve them? Do we want to teach our children to solve them?"

Only after you have read the assignment, do the following exercises in preparation for the next meeting of your group.

Learning How

Learning to solve problems and assume responsibility is not a smooth-flowing process but one that is normally filled with the ups and downs of trial and error in learning how. One way to view it is as the process of a child's giving up dependency and taking on responsibility. The following diagram illustrates a typical pattern of growth.

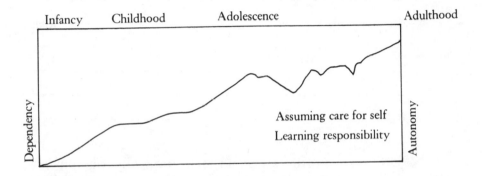

The ideal way to learn how to be responsible, as a child, is to tackle a problem, getting support and encouragement from parents who are alert to affirm our efforts, to help us evaluate the outcome and, if we fail, to urge us to try, try again. Do you recall how it was for you in learning to tie your shoelaces, ride a bike, drive a car?

1. Visualize yourself as a child and write down some of the other things you learned to do as you grew._____

   _____

   _____

29

2. What do you recall about specific responsibilities that were given to you?

| | | HOW YOU | |
THE RESPONSIBILITY	YOUR AGE	WERE PREPARED	HOW REWARDED

3. Negatives are usually said loud and clear, with vigorous enforcement, while positives often fall like raindrops, making little sound. Which do you remember most clearly: negative or positive responses? What were some words you heard most? _____

4. Who modeled responsibility for you? How? _____

5. What could have been more helpful? _____

_____

_____

6. What recent problems have you faced and taken responsibility
   for? _____

_____

_____

7. What steps did you take in the process? _____

_____

_____

8. What rewards did you experience? _____

_____

_____

Resources for the Road

> *At every moment you choose yourself. But do you choose your
> self? Body and soul contain a thousand possibilities out of which
> you can build many I's. But in only one of them is there a
> congruence of the elector and the elected. Only one—which you
> will never find until you have excluded all those superficial and
> fleeting possibilities of being and doing with which you toy, out
> of curiosity or wonder or greed, and which hinder you from*

31

*casting anchor in the experience of the mystery of life, and the
consciousness of the talent entrusted to you which is your I.*

DAG HAMMARSKJÖLD,
Markings

Peck refers, on page 43, to Allen Wheelis's book *How People
Change* (Harper & Row: 1973). In the chapter "Freedom and Necessity," Wheelis argues that there is a realm of life for all of us in
which some feel under obligation to give in to forces they think to
be *outside* of themselves but which are really *inside* them and therefore under their control. For others, there is freedom to make
choices and changes. One man sees himself stuck in a job, a marriage, an impasse, until he sees other people in the same circumstances changing and realizes the "necessity" is of his own making
and not imposed upon him.

Throughout our lives the proportion of "necessity" to "freedom"
depends upon our tolerance of conflict. The more we are threat-
ened, the more we renounce our freedom and blame our actions
on external "necessity." ("I can't because . . .") As we give up
our freedom and expand this realm of "necessity," we relieve ourselves not only of conflict but also of authority and significance.

There are things we *cannot* do, but they are fewer than we tend
to think. Knowing our bounds, we can accept them and, turning
away from them, live in our freedom. However small our realm of
freedom, acting on it can expand it to occupy the whole of the
significance of our lives.

Where are you feeling bound by necessity? _____

_____

_____

What areas of freedom for change do you need to explore, to exercise? _____

_____

_____

> *Adulthood is marked by a gradual increase in one's awareness of personal impact on and effectiveness within one's world. Adults know themselves to be agents and initiators. A first realization that "I can make a difference" is part of the exuberance of the young adult. With middle adulthood comes the awareness that this personal agency is accompanied by personal responsibility. Both accountability (I am responsible for what I have done) and care (I have responsibility for what I have created) come into perspective. . . .*
>
> *But creativity is not yet generativity. The challenge of the generative stage is not only "Can I, will I produce in the larger social world?"—not even "Can I, will I be creative in my productivity?" The generativity question is "Can I, will I be responsible in nurturing life?"*
>
> EVELYN EATON WHITEHEAD
> and JAMES D. WHITEHEAD,
> *Christian Life Patterns*

Both the Jewish and Christian Scriptures are replete with examples of people who wrestle with responsibility thrust upon them, who do not run away and who, in the process, find the meaning of their lives.

Moses (in Exodus 3:1–4:17) tries at first to avoid the call to lead the Israelites out of Egypt. "Who am I, that I should go to Pharaoh?" he asks. "Oh, Lord, please send someone else to do it." But he goes when he is assured of God's presence with him and is given Aaron to be his mouthpiece.

The "children of Israel" at the border of the Promised Land (Numbers 13, 14) send in "spies" to explore the land. They conclude that it is impossible to succeed in its conquest. Two bring in a minority report, admitting the great difficulty, but concluding, "We should go up and take possession of the land, for we can certainly do it."

Jeremiah resists his call at first: "Oh, Sovereign Lord, I do not know how to speak. I am only a child." But he responds at last (Jeremiah 1:4–8).

Jonah fled to Tarshish rather than carry a message of judgment to the city of Nineveh, but, repenting, he carries out his mission.

In the New Testament, Paul is a case study in dealing with freedom and necessity in his imprisonment for preaching the Christian message. Certain things are obviously beyond his control, but within the area in which he is free to choose and act he speaks as a truly free and responsible man.

He takes comfort in the example of Jesus who voluntarily became a servant for the sake of others (Philippians 2:5–11). He counsels against complaining and arguing (2:14). He renounces power and prestige for higher values (3:4–8). He claims to have reached a state of contentment (4:11–13). And what has happened to him, he says in Philippians 1:12, has only served to advance the Gospel.

In Romans 12:1,2, Paul suggests two ways in which we can face the pressures of life: by conforming or being transformed. J. B. Phillips translates verse 2 as follows: "Don't let the world around you squeeze you into its mold, but let God re-mold you from within."

We can live "from the outside in," acquiescing to the external forces that impinge on our lives, or we can live "from the inside out," initiating action based on chosen goals and values that we

34

have internalized. In other words, we can avoid responsibility by "letting life happen," or we can take responsibility for our lives and "make life happen."

When you think of the story of your life do you feel like an observer who is reading the story, or do you feel like the author who is writing your story?

Dedication to Reality

Looking Back

You spent time in your last group session distinguishing what responsibilities are appropriately yours and which are not, on how to distinguish the two, and on a specific situation in your own life in which you may be avoiding responsibility. How do you feel now about what you learned? You may wish to make some notes about the session: What happened between people, what feelings were expressed, and what is worth remembering? Use the space to keep a record for yourself.

_____

_____

_____

_____

_____

_____

_____

_____

_____

_____

_____

_____

_____

1. What kinds of decisions do you enjoy making and what do you tend to avoid? Name a few. _____

   _____

   _____

2. Where are you now sensing the possibility of new freedom?

   _____

   _____

   _____

Looking Ahead

READING ASSIGNMENT: Read pages 44–63 in *The Road Less Traveled* and then prepare for your next group session by doing the following exercises:

Picturing Yourself

1. Find a picture of yourself as a child.

2. Choose a place where you can be quiet and undisturbed. Get comfortable, with feet on the floor, back erect. Breathe slowly, deeply. Let go of any tightness in your body. Look at the picture of yourself as a child. Let yourself *be* that child in your imagination. Visualize yourself that size again. Close your eyes and recall the house or apartment you lived in—your room, the kitchen, the yard, your neighborhood, your school, and so on.

3. When you have immersed yourself sufficiently in that world of your childhood begin to recall some of the beliefs you held then and write them down.

   What you believed about yourself: _____
   _____
   _____

   About your parents: _____
   _____
   _____

   Your siblings: _____
   _____
   _____

   Your place in the family: _____
   _____

_____

_____

In the neighborhood: _____

_____

_____

In school: _____

_____

_____

4. How were your beliefs the same, or different, from those of your parents? Your siblings? Your peers? _____

_____

_____

Dr. Eric Berne, the psychiatrist who developed Transactional Analysis, once wrote, "On the basis of early experience with the breast, the bottle, in the bedroom, kitchen and living room the child acquires his convictions, makes his decision and takes his position. Then from what he hears he chooses a prediction and a plan: how he will go about being a winner or a loser, on what grounds and what the payoff will be. . . . The plan he makes for the eternal future is drawn to the family specification."

5. How is this true of you? _____

_____

_____

(If you have time and wish to do so, find another picture of yourself, this time as a teenager, live back into your experience and feelings during that period of your life and record what your beliefs were, just as you did for your childhood.) ———

———————————————————————

———————————————————————

———————————————————————

6. Identify some beliefs that you held as a child but have now discarded: ——————————————————

———————————————————————

———————————————————————

———————————————————————

Childhood maps of reality become so much a way of seeing our world that we need help in sorting out our beliefs, our ways of seeing reality, lest we live in self-deception.

> There is nothing worse than self-deception, where the deceiver is always with you.
> PLATO, *Dialogues*

> One is always in the dark about one's own personality. One needs others to get to know oneself.
> CARL JUNG, quoted in *Jung Speaks*

> Oh the comfort, the inexpressible comfort, of feeling safe with a person, having neither to weigh thoughts nor measure words, but to pour them all out, just as it is, chaff and grain together, knowing that a faithful friend will take and sift them, keeping what is worth keeping, and then, with the breath of kindness, blowing the rest away.
> MARY ANN EVANS (George Eliot)

The following diagram illustrates the process of coming to know oneself and being known by others:

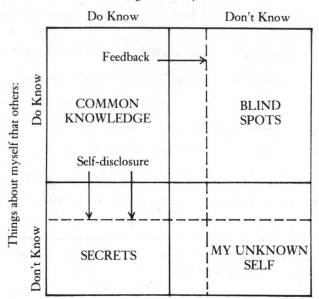

THE JO-HARI WINDOW
(So named because two men named Joe and Harry first thought of it)

The process of enlarging the area of common knowledge is accomplished by letting myself be known (self-disclosure) and by soliciting and receiving honest feedback from others.

The risks of self-disclosure are possible rejection and betrayal of trust. The rewards are greater acceptance and intimacy in human relationships and a deeper touch with reality. Security rests in one's trusting one's own worth, in trusting the acceptance of others, and ultimately in trusting the love of God who knows us completely.

7. Take some time to get acquainted with the Jo-Hari Window, then respond to these questions:

What will you risk by self-disclosure? _____

_____

_____

_____

What might you gain? _____

_____

_____

With whom have you risked (will you risk) sharing your inner realities? _____

_____

_____

Resources for the Road

Both Jewish and Christian Scriptures encourage us to live our lives openly before God and others, avoiding self-deception and illusion.

Psalm 139 is a classic statement of our inability to hide from God.

> *O Lord, you have searched me and you know me. . . .*
> *You perceive my thoughts from afar. . . .*

You are familiar with all my ways . . .
Where can I go from your Spirit?
Where can I flee from your presence?

What may seem terrifying to the psalmist, as he admits it and reflects on God's concern for his life, becomes a blanket of security which calls forth this concluding petition:

Search me, O God, and know my heart;
test me and know my anxious thoughts.
See if there be any offensive way in me,
And lead me in the way everlasting.

Surely you desire truth in the inner parts;
You teach me wisdom in the inmost place. . . .

PSALM 51:6

Do not merely listen to the word, and so deceive yourselves.
Do what it says. Anyone who listens to the word but does not
do what it says is like a man who looks at his face in a mirror
and, after looking at himself, goes away and immediately forgets
what he looks like.

JAMES 1:22–25

Speaking the truth in love . . . each of you must put off falsehood and speak truthfully to his neighbor, for we are all members of one body. . . . Live a life of love.

EPHESIANS 4:25–5:2

God is light; in him there is no darkness at all. If we claim to have fellowship with him yet walk in the darkness, we lie and do not live by the truth. But if we walk in the light, as he is in the light, we have fellowship with one another, and the blood of Jesus, his Son, purifies us from every sin.

I JOHN 1:5–7

If you and I can honestly tell each other who we are, that is, what we think, judge, feel, value, love, honor and esteem, hate, fear, desire, hope for, believe in and are committed to, then and then only can each of us grow. Then and then alone can each of us be what he really is, say what he really thinks, tell what he really feels, express what he really loves. This is the real meaning of authenticity as a person, that my exterior truly reflects my interior. It means I can be honest in the communication of my person to others. And this I cannot do unless you help me. Unless you help me, I cannot grow, or be happy, or really come alive.

I have to be free and able to say my thoughts to you, to tell you about my judgments and values, to expose you to my fears and frustrations, to admit to you my failures and my shames, to share my triumphs, before I can really be sure what it is that I am and can become. I must be able to tell you who I am before I can know who I am. And I must know who I am before I can act truly, that is, in accordance with my true self.

JOHN POWELL, S.J.,
"Why Am I Afraid to Tell You Who I Am?"

We become fully conscious only of what we are able to express to someone else. We may already have had a certain inner intuition about it, but it must remain vague so long as it is unformulated.

PAUL TOURNIER,
The Meaning of Persons

LESSON FOUR

Balancing

Looking Back

Your last group session focused on the necessity of updating our "maps of reality" as we grow out of childhood and adolescence into young and older adulthood. These maps have to do both with outer reality (the ways we view the world) and with inner reality (the ways we see ourselves) and how our willingness to disclose ourselves and welcome feedback affects our growth.

Are there issues "left over" from the session that you would like to record? How did you risk, or not risk, sharing? What feelings and desires are you left with? Take a few minutes to note them in the space provided.

_____

_____

Looking Ahead

Read pages 64–78 in *The Road Less Traveled* in which Peck argues that "discipline itself must be disciplined." Two issues come into focus: the complexity of life and the stages we must pass through in our growth toward maturity.

BALANCING Life's complexity confronts us with few "either-ors" but rather the necessity "to strike and continually restrike a delicate balance between conflicting needs, goals, duties, directions." Thus the tools we have already discussed call for constant adjustment.

Delaying Gratification

Delay_____Spontaneity

Accepting Responsibility

Over-responsible_____Under-responsible

Dedication to Reality

Totally honest_____Withholding

1. Imagine that you are a tightrope walker in training, daily trying to keep your balance between conflicting needs, goals, duties, directions. List some of the tensions you feel in the space below. For example:

   Time for yourself _____ Time for others

   _____
   _____
   _____
   _____
   _____

GIVING UP The "stages of life," so eloquently described by Harvard University psychiatrist Erik Erikson,* are like a stairway to be climbed in our journey to maturity. Each step requires the giving up of resting in the security of the past step. Thus, to be born is to give up the comfort and security of the womb.

2. Where are you on the stairway of life? And what are some of the things you have attained? What have you had to give up to grow up? Draw yourself where you think you are on the stairway and make some notes regarding what you have attained and given up in order to get there.

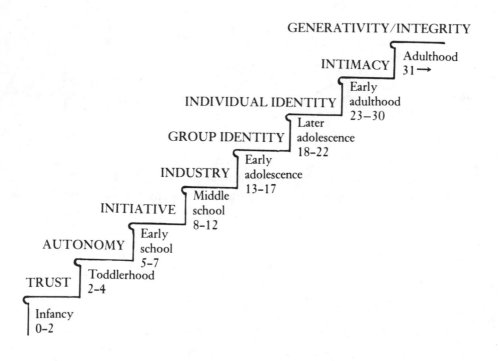

* See pages 56–57 for a fuller description of life's stages, based on Erikson's research.

3. A temporary form of giving up is what Peck calls "bracketing." It is putting oneself aside, silencing the familiar, and welcoming the strange, the new. Close your eyes and look back over the past week in search of a time when you did this. Make some notes on the experience.

I bracketed _____

_____

_____

I learned _____

_____

_____

4. Where do I need to gain new perspective? _____

_____

_____

5. How can I? _____

_____

_____

_____

6. What stands in my way? _____

_____

_____

_____

Robert Raines writes, in *Living the Questions*, "We can't go home again. We can't recapture our lost innocence. We can't go back to patterns of feeling and behavior that suited us yesterday. For it is today, and today creates its own urgencies and choices. Nostalgia is real, but it is not reality. We have suffered loss from yesterday even as we bring its gain into today. We can't go home again because people and places change. 'The old gray mare ain't what she used to be,' and neither are we—for better and for worse.

"And yet we can always go home again. Though we may leave home, home never leaves us. Though we stay home, we may never discover what home is until we leave it. Home has to do with our continuities—as persons and as a nation and as creatures on homeland earth. Home is those people and places which nourish our identity and vocation. Home consists of those roots and sources from which the energies of faith, hope and love pour forth. Home is where the meaning flows, where the heart goes. Home is 'something you haven't to deserve.' Home is given and forgiven. Home is 'wherever the sensibility can defend itself, where humanness can begin to rediscover its outlines against a backdrop of ruins.' We can lose home and we can choose home. Home happens where and when we feel at home—in the universe, in our communities of significance, with ourselves. Home has to do with our communities."

7. Where are you "at home"? _____

_____

_____

8. How are you fed and strengthened for the next part of your journey? _____

_____

_____

_____

_____

_____

_____

_____

Resources for the Road

Unless we cop out in some way, the challenge to bring more of ourselves into life is the healthiest kind of problem we can have. It looks different at different ages—a boy learns to be a friend and then to be a husband and a father and it is not ended then—each stage has a cluster of challenges that demand something more of him that is clean and true. We go through life mining our own resources, building new dimensions of ourselves on the structures we have just laid down. The everyday problems come in connection with growing. These are always invitations to develop and come to grips with the difficulties that each new moment presents. We don't really get through life by solving problems in a final way but by responding more adequately as we move along.

EUGENE KENNEDY,
Living with Everyday Problems

In the New Testament, Jesus' message hinges on the paradoxical assertion that we must die in order to live. Thus in Matthew 16:25 he is recorded as having said, "Whoever wants to save his life will lose it, but whoever loses his life for me will find it." (See also Matthew 10:39, Mark 8:35, Luke 9:24 and John 12:24,25.) To Ni-

53

codemus, the teacher of the law, Jesus said, "You must be born anew" (John 3:7).

Paul is an example of giving up to grow up. In I Corinthians 13:11 he said, "When I was a child, I talked like a child, I thought like a child, I reasoned like a child. When I became a man, I put childish ways behind me."

The apostle Peter urged his readers to "rid yourselves of all malice and deceit, hypocrisy, envy, and slander of every kind. Like newborn babies, crave pure spiritual milk, so that by it you may grow up in your salvation" (I Peter 2:1,2).

> *There are opposites within us, call them what we like—masculine and feminine, anima and animus, Yin and Yang—and these are eternally in tension and are eternally seeking to unite. The human soul is a great arena in which the Active and the Receptive, the Light and the Dark, the Yang and the Yin, seek to come together and forge within us an indescribable unity of personality. To achieve this union of the opposites within ourselves may very well be the task of life, requiring the utmost in perseverance and assiduous awareness. . . . The desire of the soul to unite with consciousness and forge an indivisible and creative personality is the most powerful urge within us. On this level, the urge toward wholeness and the urge to find God are identical, and so this urge to wholeness and individuation is also called by Jung the religious instinct.*
>
> JOHN A. SANFORD,
> *The Invisible Partners*

Erikson stresses the developmental character of much in adult experience. There are several points central to Erikson's understanding:

1. There is available to each person a range of psychological strengths and resources. These resources are based in the genetic makeup of the human species and thus, in one sense, "given" for each individual from conception. At the start of life these strengths exist in potential. Only gradually over the course of one's life are these resources realized as consistent characteristics of the personality. The process of the unfolding of the personality does not only occur in infancy or through adolescence but continues over the entire life span. There are, in fact, aspects of the personality which are developed in consistent personal strengths only in the mature years.

2. There is a pattern to be seen in this unfolding, a normal, expectable sequence to the process through which the resources of the personality are called forth. . . .

3. The emergence of each new psychological resource or strength marks a critical time for the individual, a decisive moment in personal development. At a point in an individual's life a particular concern becomes central. This concern raises a significant question to the person, challenges the current state of one's life and one's level of self-understanding. The resolution of this challenge will require a judgment, a choice, a decisive action that will carry important implications for what follows in one's life. As a result of this encounter with myself, I will be different—whether I accept the challenge and move through it to a more confident possession of personality strengths or back away from the challenge and refuse (from fear or lack of support) to face the question it raises about myself.

4. The self-confrontation provoked by each of these developmental challenges will put the individual in contact with contradictory impulses and with both positive and negative aspects of the personality. The resolution that Erikson suggests is not the unwavering suppression of the negative impulse nor an aggressive dominance by the positive. At

any stage, maturity is achieved through a blending of these ambiguous dimensions in a "favorable ratio," a personally appropriate synthesis that is true to one's history and personality. Such a synthesis produces a consistent psychological strength that fits into and completes the character of the individual.

EVELYN EATON WHITEHEAD and
JAMES D. WHITEHEAD,
Christian Life Patterns

The Stages of Life

LIFE STAGE	DEVELOPMENTAL TASKS	GROWTH CRISIS
1. INFANCY Birth to 2 years	1. Social attachment 2. Object permanence 3. Sensorimotor intelligence and causality 4. Maturation of motor functions	TRUST VS. MISTRUST
2. TODDLERHOOD 2–4 years	1. Self-control 2. Language development 3. Fantasy and play 4. Elaboration of locomotion	AUTONOMY VS. SHAME AND DOUBT
3. EARLY SCHOOL 5–7 years	1. Sex role identification 2. Early moral development 3. Concrete operations 4. Group play	INITIATIVE VS. GUILT
4. MIDDLE SCHOOL 8–12 years	1. Social cooperation 2. Self-evaluation 3. Skill learning 4. Team play	INDUSTRY VS. INFERIORITY

5. EARLY ADOLESCENCE 13–17 years	1. Physical maturation 2. Formal operations 3. Membership in peer group 4. Heterosexual relations	GROUP IDENTITY vs. ALIENATION
6. LATER ADOLESCENCE 18–22 years	1. Autonomy from parents 2. Sex role identity 3. Internalized morality 4. Career choices	INDIVIDUAL IDENTITY vs. ROLE DIFFUSION
7. EARLY ADULTHOOD 23–30 years	1. Work 2. Life-style 3. Marriage 4. Childbearing	INTIMACY vs. ISOLATION
8. MIDDLE ADULTHOOD 31–50 years	1. Management of career 2. Management of household 3. Child-rearing	GENERATIVITY vs. STAGNATION
9. LATER ADULTHOOD 51 years	1. Redirection of energy to new roles 2. Acceptance of one's life 3. Acceptance of one's death	INTEGRITY vs. DESPAIR

On Love

Looking Back

In your last session you dealt with two issues: the tensions within which we all live that require flexible responses to keep our balance and the stages of life that require us to give up securities of the past in order to move on into the future. What happened in the group meeting? Are there feelings, issues, insights you wish to record? Use the space provided.

_____

_____

_____

_____

_____

Looking Ahead

Read pages 81–97 in *The Road Less Traveled*, then do the following exercises in preparation for your next session:

1. Close the book and write, in your own words, a paraphrase of Peck's definition of what love isn't:_____

_____

_____

_____

_____

and what love is: _____

_____

_____

   Now look at the book and check to see how well you grasped his meaning.

2. Mark each of the following statements as to whether it is true or false.

TRUE FALSE

1. ☐ ☐ Love of self and love of others become indistinguishable.
2. ☐ ☐ The act of loving is an act of self-evolution.
3. ☐ ☐ We are incapable of loving another unless we love ourselves.
4. ☐ ☐ Love becomes real only through exertion.
5. ☐ ☐ Ego boundaries provide safety.
6. ☐ ☐ Ego boundaries create loneliness.
7. ☐ ☐ The experience of falling in love is an act of regression.
8. ☐ ☐ The work of loving begins when one falls out of love.
9. ☐ ☐ Falling in love is in fact very, very close to real love.
10. ☐ ☐ The more we love the more blurred becomes the distinction between ourselves and the world.

3. Compare and contrast the experiences of falling in love and mystical union in terms of the following aspects (see Peck, p. 95–7):

	FALLING IN LOVE	MYSTICAL UNION
Ego boundaries:		
Inclusive of:		
Duration of:		
Results of:		
Which is peak; which is plateau?		
Extent/place of real loving:		

4. What old beliefs or messages about love do I need to give up in order to grow toward true loving? _____
_____
_____

5. What balancing do I need in order to love more effectively?

_____

_____

_____

_____

Resources for the Road

Love asks people to become more of their true selves in each other's presence and to become more steadily alive and sensitive to each other's person.

EUGENE KENNEDY,
Living with Everyday Problems

In love, the gates of my soul spring open,
Allowing me to breathe a new air of freedom
and forget my own petty self.
In love, my whole being streams forth
out of the rigid confines of
narrowness and self-assertion,
which makes me a prisoner
of my own poverty and emptiness.

KARL RAHNER

One psychotherapist who admires *The Road Less Traveled* nonetheless takes issue with Peck's definition of love. "I think he misses something important by using the word *extend*," John Fortunato writes in his book, *Embracing the Exile*. "I would use the word *transcend*. Love means 'transcending one's self for the purpose of nurturing . . .

another's spiritual growth.' " In so doing, Fortunato points to the divine source of true love.

We are meant to love people and use things, not love things and use people.

"Love comes from God . . . because God is love," we read in I John 4:7,8, and in so saying the New Testament writer uses a Greek word, *agape*, that expresses unconditional, self-giving love. God "wills to extend himself" toward us for no reason other than that God loves all the creation, especially those of us who are made in "the image of God" and can respond and become agents of love in the world.

"For God so loved the world that He gave . . ." (John 3:16).

"A new commandment I give you," Jesus said, "that you love one another as I have loved you" (John 13:34,35).

"Greater love has no man than this, that a man lay down his life for his friends" (John 15:12,13).

"Love must be sincere. . . . Be devoted to one another. . . . Honor one another above yourselves. . . . Share with God's people who are in need. Practice hospitality. . . . Live in harmony with one another. . . . Overcome evil with good" (Romans 12:9–21).

"Love is patient, love is kind.
It does not envy, it does not boast, it is not proud.
It is not rude, it is not self-seeking, it is not easily angered; it keeps no record of wrongdoings.
It always protects, always trusts, always hopes, always perseveres.

Love never fails" (I Corinthians 13:4–8).

"You are called to be free. But do not use your freedom to indulge your sinful nature; rather, serve one another in love. The entire law is summed up in a single command: 'Love your neighbor as yourself' " (Galatians 5:13).

"Keep the royal law found in Scripture: 'Love your neighbor as yourself' " (James 2:8).

"We ought to lay down our lives for our brothers. . . . Dear children, let us not love with words or tongue but with actions and in truth" (I John 3:16,18).

Beneath and above the shifting sands of time, the uncertainties that darken our days, and the vicissitudes that cloud our nights is a wise and loving God. This universe is not a tragic expression of meaningless chaos but a marvelous display of orderly cosmos. . . . Man is not a wisp of smoke from a limitless smoldering, but a child of God created "a little lower than the angels." Above the manyness of time stands the one eternal God, with wisdom to guide us, strength to protect us, and love to keep us. His boundless love supports and contains us as a mighty ocean contains and supports the tiny drops of every wave. With a surging fullness He is forever moving toward us, seeking to fill the creeks and bays of our lives with unlimited resources.

MARTIN LUTHER KING,
The Strength to Love

The agonizing moments through which I have passed during the last few years have also drawn me closer to God. More than ever before I am convinced of the reality of a personal God. True, I have always believed in the personality of God. But in the past the idea of a personal God was little more than a metaphysical category that I found theologically and philosophically satisfying. Now it is a living reality that has been validated in the experiences of everyday life. God has been profoundly real to me in recent years. In the midst of lonely days, and dreary nights I have heard an inner voice saying, "Lo, I will be with you." When the chains of fear and the manacles of frustration have all but stymied my efforts, I have felt the power of God transforming the fatigue of despair into the buoyancy of hope. I am convinced that the universe is under the control of a loving purpose, and that in the struggle for righteousness man has cosmic companionship. Behind the harsh appearances of the world there is a benign power.

MARTIN LUTHER KING,
The Strength to Love

If I truly love one person,
  I love all persons,
  I love the world,
  I love life.
If I say to somebody else,
  "I love you,"
I must be able to say,
  "I love in you everybody,
  I love through you the world,
  I love in you also myself."

ERICH FROMM

What Love Isn't and Is

Looking Back

In your last session you were introduced to what Peck says is the motive and energy for disciplining ourselves: love. Admitting that no one can define love adequately, Peck nonetheless offers his definition. He differentiates true love from "falling in love," "romantic love," and "cathecting," a word he uses to describe becoming attached to a person or object.

What do you wish to record as a permanent record of that meeting? You are now halfway through the 12-session course. How do you feel at this point? What is happening to you? Use the space provided.

_____

_____

_____
_____
_____
_____
_____
_____
_____
_____
_____
_____

Looking Ahead

Read pages 98–131 in *The Road Less Traveled* and spend some time on the following exercises in preparation for your next group session.

1. We are often confused and have difficulty distinguishing real love from counterfeits. Here is an exercise in sorting out the characteristics of real love from ones frequently mistaken for the real thing. Check whether these statements are true or false.

T   F

____ ____   a. Love is the free exercise of choice.

____ ____   b. Two people love each other only when they are quite capable of living without each other.

____ ____   c. Loving is the inability to experience wholeness or to function adequately without the certainty that one is being cared for by another.

___   ___   d. A desire for the growing independence of the other is one of the signs of real love.

___   ___   e. When you love somebody you want to "make them happy."

___   ___   f. Needing someone means really loving them.

___   ___   g. Real love just comes spontaneously and naturally, without effort.

___   ___   h. If a mother has strong enough feelings for her infant she will have no problem with loving him.

___   ___   i. We can only genuinely love human beings to whom we are naturally attracted.

___   ___   j. Real loving is often painful.

___   ___   k. Real love is always self-fulfilling.

___   ___   l. Withholding is often just as important as giving.

___   ___   m. Falling out of love may precede real loving.

___   ___   n. Genuine love is volitional and judicious rather than emotional.

___   ___   o. Love is both selfish and non-selfish.

2. "Love is as love *does*." What loving have you *done* this week? ___

_____

_____

3. "Love is a two way street—the giver always receives." What receiving have you done this week? _____

_____

_____

When Peck moves on to what love *is*, he describes it as always either work or courage. The principal form that the work of love takes is *attention*. And the most important way we exercise our attention is by listening.

Here are some guidelines for true listening:

    a. Notice the attitudes and feelings involved as well as a person's words. Be aware of "body language" and what it is saying.

    b. Seek to understand the feelings expressed, accepting them as legitimate and neither denying nor minimizing them.

    c. Listen for what a person is *not* saying as well as what is said.

    d. Check out what you are hearing by telling a person as exactly as you can what you heard said, together with the attitudes and feelings you heard expressed. Try to use words different from the other person's without changing the meaning expressed.

    e. *Do not* respond with your own message by evaluating, sympathizing, giving your opinion, offering advice, analyzing or questioning. Simply report back what you heard in the message, the attitudes and the feelings that were expressed.

4. In the light of these guidelines, how much time have you spent in really listening to others this week? When did you experience the "duet dance" of listening? _____

_____

_____

_____

5. What blocks you from really listening to others? _____

_____

_____

Resources for the Road

Communication is:

How to talk so others will listen;
How to listen so others will talk;
How to understand so love can win.

Without honesty there is no truth;
Without truth there is no understanding;
Without understanding there is no love;
Without love there is nothing.

Communication means living in open relation to the past, present, and future. This requires being open to people through:

1. LISTENING: Cultivating the ability to *hear* with the expectation of learning, of increasing our knowledge, sharpening our values, broadening and strengthening our convictions.

Accurate listening requires use of feedback:
"Is this what you mean?"
"I hear you saying . . . Is that what you mean?"
"Am I hearing you right?"

2. SPEAKING: Learning to report to others what is going on inside of me.

Are my words true to my feelings?
Are my words appropriate to the situation?
Are my words considerate of the person hearing me?

3. UNDERSTANDING: It opens up the possibility of our accepting another person. When a person is able to feel and communicate genuine acceptance of another, he/she possesses the capacity for being a powerful helping agent for the other. Acceptance of the other, as he or she is, is a powerful factor in freeing the other person to make constructive changes, learning to solve problems and realize their true potential.

HOW DOES ACCURATE LISTENING HELP?
1. It helps people free themselves of troublesome feelings by expressing them openly.
2. It helps people become less afraid of negative feelings.
3. It helps promote a feeling of understanding between and among people.
4. It helps to facilitate problem solving.
5. It helps to keep the ownership of the problem with the person involved in the problem.
6. It helps to try to hear what people are *not* saying, what they perhaps will never be able to say, but are feeling and need to express.

How beautiful, how grand and liberating this experience is, when people learn to help each other. It is impossible to overemphasize the immense need humans have to be really listened to, to be taken seriously, to be understood.

Modern psychology has brought it very much to our attention. At the very heart of all psychotherapy is this type of relationship in which one can tell everything, just as a little child will tell all to his mother.

No one can develop freely in this world and find a full life without feeling understood by at least one person. . . .

He who would see himself clearly must open up to a confidant freely chosen and worthy of such trust.

PAUL TOURNIER, M.D.

The speaker in the presence of a human listener is never unaware of the judgment of what the listener is upon his life, and in turn, the listener's own life cannot resist the judging effect of what the speaker is on his own life. Here are fields of radiation that interpenetrate each other and that leave neither party unprobed. Nietzsche declares, "In one's friend, one shall have one's best enemy," an enemy that rebukes and judges that which is inauthentic in the friend.

In the listener, then, if he be a true friend, a true listener, there is inevitably an enemy to much that is in the speaker. But this "enemy" in the listener is not the re-introduction of any level of conscious judgment, any weakening of the listener's complete acceptance of the speaker. This enemy is an effortless, unconscious influence which rises up out of what the listener is in what he does.

It may be all very well to say as Nietzsche does that "many a one cannot loosen his own fetters, but is nevertheless his friend's emancipator." But the odds are heavily against such a miracle. For it is only the listener whose own fetters, if not shattered, have at least been loosed, who seems able effortlessly to irradiate the level of existence of the speaker in such a way as to move him toward release. Any minimizing of the maturity required of the listener may lead to the most tragic conse-

73

quences. Furthermore it is only the mature listener who without disturbing the listening situation can submit both humbly and fearlessly to the counter radiation of the speaker to which he is continuously subjected.

Yet even this does not seem to get to the bottom of the matter. . . . It leaves out of all account the living Listener who "stands behind our lattices and waits." It ignores the hidden Presence, the patient, all-penetrating Listener, the third member of every conversation, whose very existence, if it is not ignored, rebukes and damps down the evil, and calls out and underlies the good, drawing from the visible participants things they did not know they possessed.

It does this not in a conspicuous fashion, as an orchestra leader tones down the brass with a menacing downstroke of his baton or calls forth the strings with a beckoning upward gesture, but does it more like the quietly permeating influence of a person of patent purity sitting silently in a conversation, saying almost nothing, but whose presence there changes all.

Douglas V. Steere,
On Listening to Another

The Courage of Love

Looking Back

Your last session distinguished true love from dependency, from cathecting, from self-sacrifice and from mere feeling. And you focused on the commonest and most important way to give attention to another; *listening*. Make a record of the most important things that happened to you in the session and the feelings you are left with, how you *really* listened and how you were *really* listened to.

_____

_____

_____

_____

_____

_____

_____

_____

_____

_____

_____

_____

_____

Looking Ahead

Read pages 131–55 in *The Road Less Traveled* and prepare for your next group session by reflecting on the following questions:

Peck says, "Courage is not the absence of fear; it is the making of action in spite of fear, the moving out against the resistance engendered by fear into the unknown and into the future" (p. 131). "Thus all life itself represents a risk, and the more lovingly we live our lives the more risks we take" (p. 134).

The Risks of Love

1. On the chart below note where you are in your own venturing, by filling in specifics. (For more space, reproduce the chart on a separate sheet of paper.)

THE RISK	HOW I AVOIDED IT	HOW I FACED IT
Loss		
Growing Up		
Commitment		
Confrontation		

2. What losses have been most difficult for you to face? _____

_____

_____

3. How have you grown in love through facing a loss? _____

_____

_____

4. What "leaps" into adulthood have you taken? _____
_____
_____

5. In what way were you loving yourself in taking these leaps?
_____
_____

6. What relationships of constancy (or commitment) have you experienced? _____
_____
_____

7. How have they contributed to your growth? _____

_____

_____

Peck says, "It is impossible to truly understand another without making room for that person within yourself, . . . which . . . requires an extension of and therefore a changing of the self" (p. 149).

8. Close your eyes and focus attention on your breathing. Relax and let your mind become like a movie screen. Now let a picture come into focus of some person whom you wish to understand and love. See that person as separate and unique. Then see yourself making room within yourself for that very uniqueness. How are you needing to extend yourself in real life for this to become true? _____

_____

_____

9. How are you feeling about such a commitment? _____

_____

_____

_____

_____

10. Picture yourself confronting this person about some difference or conflict, and in turn being confronted by them. What feelings does this bring up in you? _____

_____

_____

Resources for the Road

Fear of life leads to excessive fear of death. . . . In some way one must pay with life and consent daily to die, to give oneself up to the risks and dangers of the world, allow oneself to be engulfed and used up. Otherwise one ends up as though dead in trying to avoid life and death.

ERNEST BECKER,
The Denial of Death

To laugh is to risk appearing the fool.
To weep is to risk appearing sentimental.
To reach out is to risk involvement.
To expose feelings is to risk exposing your true self.
To place your ideas and dreams before the crowd is to risk their love.
To love is to risk not being loved in return.
To live is to risk dying.
To hope is to risk despair.
To try is to risk failure.
But the greatest hazard in life is to risk nothing.
The one who risks nothing does nothing and has nothing—and finally is nothing.
He may avoid sufferings and sorrow,
But he simply cannot learn, feel, change, grow or love.
Chained by his certitude, he is a slave; he has forfeited freedom.
Only one who risks is free!

AUTHOR UNKNOWN

The Bible speaks clearly to the risks of loving.

THE RISK OF LOSS Jesus warned of the risks in following him. To those who promised to follow, he said, "Foxes have holes and birds of the air have nests, but the Son of Man has no place to lay his head" (Luke 9:58). "Whoever wants to save his life will lose it" (Luke 9:24).

Paul the apostle talked frankly of the risks he took in his spiritual journey: "Whatever was to my profit I now consider loss for the sake of Christ," he wrote, "for whose sake I have lost all things" (Philippians 3:7,8).

"The Lord gave, and the Lord has taken away," Job exclaimed, "may the name of the Lord be praised" (Job 1:21).

THE RISK OF INDEPENDENCE Jesus encouraged independent thinking when he asked, "Why don't you judge for yourselves what is right?" (Luke 12:57).

And Paul said, "Each one should test his own actions. Then he can take pride in himself . . . for each one should carry his own load" (Galatians 6:4,5).

THE RISK OF COMMITMENT Joshua challenged the Israelites as they were about to enter the Promised Land, to make up their minds what their commitment would be, whether to the Lord or to other gods, concluding, "Choose for yourselves this day whom you will serve" (Joshua 24:15).

Jesus insisted, "No one can serve two masters" (Matthew 6:24), and urged his hearers to "enter by the narrow gate . . . for the gate is narrow, and the way is hard, that leads to life, and those who find it are few" (Matthew 7:13,14).

Underlying all this, however, is the assurance of God's commitment to those who trust him, in references almost too numerous to mention. But here is a sampling:

"God is our refuge and strength, a very present help in trouble" (Psalm 46:1).

"If God is for us, who is against us? . . . For I am sure that [nothing] in all creation, will be able to separate us from the love of God that is in Christ Jesus our Lord" (Romans 8:31–39).

"God has said, 'I will never fail you nor forsake you' " (Hebrews 13:5).

"I know whom I have believed, and am convinced that he is able to guard what I have entrusted to him" (II Timothy 1:12).

THE RISK OF CONFRONTATION Jesus gave careful instructions on how to deal with situations needing confrontation.

"If your brother sins against you, go and show him his fault, just between the two of you. . . . But if he will not listen, take one or two others along, so that 'every matter may be established by the testimony of two or three witnesses' " (Matthew 18:15,16).

Paul the apostle wrote two extremely confrontive letters to the church in Corinth and struggled with "how to be loving" in doing so. You may read of his anguish in II Corinthians 1:12–2:4: "I wrote you out of great distress and anguish of heart and with many tears, not to grieve you but to let you know the depth of my love for you."

> *Something in us does not believe we can survive fundamental changes in personality structure or life circumstances and so crisis in life is shadowed by death. Then when we survive the crisis we realize that change may mean metamorphosis rather than death. The ego dies and a stronger self is born. Then it may come to us that death is only a gateway to wider life, the final trip beyond the prison of the ego.*
>
> SAM KEEN, ANNE VALLEY FOX,
> *Telling Your Story*

82

Change always is precious, comes slowly, and has a high cost. It can give the appearance of having occurred at one breathless juncture, but on the way to every peak moment are plateau stretches where it will seem to us that we work without any return for our labour. Those stretches make possible the specific occasions we can pinpoint as places of change.

So often the resolve to do better meets with consistent failure. The outcome is discouragement. We despair that we can ever be different, and may grow to dislike ourselves. Actually our broken resolves offer material germane to meditation. . . . Acceptance leads to understanding, and understanding leads to change. . . . Meditation on our responses to persons and events can be a powerful tool in our striving to be free persons. . . . The practice of meditation can give us a feeling of separation from what we are observing in ourselves. The gate is then opened for the comprehending that transforms feelings, or that takes them and returns them to us as manageable forces.

ELIZABETH O'CONNOR,
Search for Silence

The Discipline of Love

Looking Back

You focused, in your last session, on four risks of loving: loss, growing up, commitment and confrontation. Which risk made you feel most uncomfortable? What was the greatest challenge you received from the meeting? Take a few minutes to record your feelings and learnings as you look back over the group meeting.

_____

_____

_____

_____

_____

_____

_____

_____

_____

_____

_____

_____

_____

Looking Ahead

Read pages 155–82 in *The Road Less Traveled*, then spend some time responding to the following questions as you look ahead to your next session.

Peck says, "Feelings are the source of one's energy, power," but feelings need to be disciplined, and "the art of self-discipline is like the art of slave-owning." What kind of a slave-owner are you?

List some of the feelings you've experienced this week in the left-hand column below, then check what your response was to each feeling.

FEELING	HOW DID I EXPRESS IT?	HOW DID I SUPPRESS IT? WHY?	WITH WHAT RESULTS?

Look over your list and decide what kind of feelings you welcome and which are suspect. _____

_____

_____

Which feelings do you banish, or try to banish, from your life?

_____

_____

_____

_____

Select one unwelcome feeling and imagine that you are personifying it and welcoming it into your life. Write what you might say to this feeling, explaining why you have been leery of it, but why

87

you now want to experiment with a new attitude of respect and nurture. _____

_____

_____

_____

_____

_____

Now write out a response from this hitherto unwelcome feeling to its being admitted. What contributions could it make to your life, to your power to love? _____

_____

_____

_____

_____

_____

How can I be in control of this feeling rather than let it control me? _____

_____

_____

_____

Here is a helpful formula to experiment with:

Claim it; Name it; Tame it; Aim it.

Resources for the Road

Only to the self-disciplined person can one say, "Do as you will, and it will probably be all right."

ABRAHAM MASLOW

A good marriage is that in which each appoints the other guardian of his solitude. Once the realization is accepted that between the closest human beings infinite distances continue to exist, a wonderful living side by side can grow up, if they succeed in loving the distance between them which makes it possible for each to see the other whole against a wide sky.

RAINER MARIA RILKE

To renew the personal one should be able to look at a person at different times during the day, and each and every time see a different face.

THOMAS FOGARTY,
Emptiness and Closeness

To get close, one must remove the fix you have on a person, realizing that you don't know and never will know them.

To care for another person, in the most significant sense, is to help them grow and actualize themselves. . . . Caring is the antithesis of using the other person to satisfy one's own needs. The true meaning of caring is not to be confused with such meanings as wishing them well, liking, comforting and maintaining, or simply having an interest in what happens to another. Caring is a process which has a way of ordering other activities and values around itself. . . . When I truly care, as far as I am able, I promote and safeguard conditions that make my caring possible, I exclude what is incompatible with my caring, and I subordinate what is irrelevant.

Such ordering requires giving up certain things and activities, and may seem like submission. But this submission is basically liberating and affirming like the voluntary submission of the craftsman to his discipline and the requirement of his materials. It is like being liberated as the result of accepting some truth I have long tried to avoid. This submission entails giving up pretensions and coming to accept myself as I really am; I come to see the conditions of life as they are instead of as I wish them to be. . . . We are "in place" in the world through having our lives ordered by such caring. . . .

I will call those I care for "appropriate others." They are not ready made and waiting for me. They must be developed in relation to me to the point where, in conjunction with other carings, they have become the center around which my life can be significantly ordered. In helping them grow I myself am transformed; in finding and developing my appropriate others I find and create myself, and I discover and create the meaning of my life.

No one else can give me the meaning of my life; it is something I alone can make. The meaning is not something predetermined which simply unfolds; I help both to create it and to discover it in a continuing process, not a once and for all.

> MILTON MAYEROFF,
> *On Caring*

When men and women are in love, they share the mistaken belief that they live in the same world. When they "love" one another they acknowledge that they live in different worlds, but are prepared once in a while to cross the chasm between them.

> THOMAS SZASZ,
> *Heresies*

Agape love is Christ-like love. It is love of our neighbor because he too is a creature of God. It is disinterested, uncalculated, impartial, unmerited goodwill to every person. Its characteristics are as follows:

1) A sense of awe and mystery at another person;

2) The ability to see the potential of the other and to believe that this potential can be realized;

3) The ability to give oneself in appropriate ways to a particular person in a particular situation (this requires discrimination and sensitivity);

4) Helping the other to develop his potential, evoking his gifts by listening, observing, confronting, speaking the truth in love;

5) Using my own gifts, fulfilling myself, taking risks, courting the disapproval even of those we love the most and whose opinions matter most;

6) Loving a person for God's sake and not for my sake, being willing to let the other grow even though he be-

comes someone we don't like and even though he comes to be against us; and

7) Willingness to be vulnerable—to be hurt—and yet to stay with the relationship, ready to forgive and be open to the other and to new events in the situation or in the relationship.

GORDON COSBY

Some day, after we have mastered the winds, the tides, and gravity, we will harness for God the energies of love; and then for the second time in the history of the world man will have discovered fire!

PIERRE TEILHARD DE CHARDIN

In the process of reaching maturity and autonomy most of us do strive for security by trying to organize the universe around ourselves. And most of us learn only through the suffering and estrangement which attend egocentricity that this way leads not to security, but to an endlessly precarious and ultimately fruitless attempt to twist reality into meeting our private specifications. . . .

We reach our highest freedom not by asserting our own interests against the world, but by devoting ourselves in fellowship to a way of life which reaches personal fulfillment along with, and partly *through*, the fulfillment of others. We reach security only by a trustful acceptance of the full truth about ourselves and others, not by evasion of it. Healing power is latent in men because it is latent "in the nature of things." Hence it is not surprising that men and women have found in Christ the supreme disclosure of what coincidence between human beatitude and divine love means.

Christ is Saviour as He opens, for each man, the way whereby that individual can move toward such coincidence. This involves moving forward into a deepened recognition of failure, impotence and need at many points. But the divine forgiveness which He discloses always has been and always will be accessible to men. We experience divine forgiveness as that "making right" of our lives which occurs when we turn away from fighting ourselves, and others, and the truth itself, and turn trustfully toward the divine power which surrounds us and can work through us. This experience of reconciliation, despite past failures and unsolved problems in the present, makes men actually more lovable, more discerning, more capable of devoting themselves to goods which enrich all humanity.

DAVID E. ROBERTS,
Psychotherapy and a Christian View of Man

LESSON NINE

Growth and Religion

Looking Back

You discussed the discipline of feelings in your last session as well as the honoring of the separateness of one whom you love. You must have had some strong feelings about all that. What do you wish to record about the meeting, and what did you learn that you want to build into your life? Make a few notes before you go on to prepare for the next session:

_____

_____

_____

_____

_____

_____

_____

_____

_____

_____

_____

_____

_____

Looking Ahead

Read pages 185–232 in *The Road Less Traveled*. This is a longer assignment than usual, but much of it is given to record three case histories. After your reading, do the following exercises:

1. Peck says, on page 191, "The essence of a patient's childhood and hence the essence of his or her world view is captured in the 'earliest memory.' . . . I often ask, 'Tell me the very first thing that you can remember.' "

   So, close your eyes, sit comfortably, take a few deep breaths and breathe out any tiredness or reluctance you may feel to doing this exercise. Turn the clock back to your childhood—past 20,18,15 to 10,9,8,7,5,3—back as far as you can go and let your mind hover there until a memory rises to consciousness, or perhaps several of them. Choose which was your earliest memory and recall as many details as you can. Write them down, writing rapidly without editing or censoring, using the first person, present tense as you describe the event remembered. ("I am three and I am playing on the front porch," for instance.)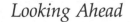

_____

_____

_____

_____

_____

_____

_____

_____

2. Look back over your account of that memory and describe your
   feelings about the nature of your existence at that time. (For
   example, you might begin, "My earliest experience of life, or
   my 'microcosm,' was . . .") _____

   _____

   _____

   _____

3. Children usually are both spiritually aware and are enthusiastic
   artists. Using crayons or paint, if you have them, make a picture
   of your earliest impressions of God. Put yourself somewhere in
   the picture. Use a separate sheet of paper if you wish.

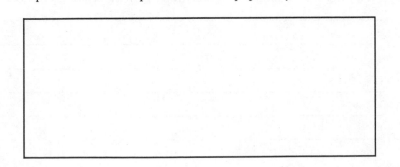

4. How has your concept of God changed? How have your feelings changed? Using symbols or words, describe God or Reality as you perceive it today: _____

_____

_____

_____

_____

5. Peck says, "The path to holiness [spiritual growth] lies through questioning *everything*" (p. 193). What have you questioned on your journey so far? _____

_____

_____

_____

What *are* you questioning? _____

_____

_____

_____

_____

6. What are your beliefs? As you think of them, write them down.

_____

_____

_____

_____

_____

_____

_____

7. "Perception of the miraculous requires no faith or assumptions. It is simply a matter of paying full and close attention to the givens of life, that is, to what is so ever-present that it is usually taken for granted" (p. 230). Observe closely what goes on within and around you this week and list at least one "miracle" you've seen each day. _____

_____

_____

_____

_____

_____

_____

_____

Resources for the Road

The new gullibility of our particular time is not that of the man who believes too much, but that of the man who believes too little—the man who has lost his sense of the miracle. When awe and wonder depart from our awareness depression sets in, and after its blanket has lain smotheringly upon us for a while, despair may ensue, or the quest for kicks begin. The loss of wonder, of awe, or the sense of the sublime, is a condition leading to the death of the soul. There is no more withering state than that which takes all things for granted. The blasé attitude means spiritual, emotional, intellectual and creative death.

EDMOND FULLER,
Man in Modern Fiction

In every age, there have been skeptics and critical minds who found anthropomorphic elements in God language abhorrent and have substituted more abstract philosophical notions—the Prime Mover, the Absolute Spirit, Nature, the Life Force, Cosmic Consciousness, Energy. But all of the capitalized nouns that appear in nontheistic visions are pseudonyms for God. They are all designed to make the existential affirmation that there is a bond between the self and cosmos, that every being is within Being, that human consciousness is interior to the consciousness that informs all things. God in His-Her-Its aliases is a cry that self makes: "I am not alone!"

SAM KEEN,
The Passionate Life

We have come to dissociate belief from faith, and we think of belief as a way of thinking, but the original intent of the language (Greek) was not to describe a way of thinking but a way of acting. Actually our English word be-lief comes from the old Anglo Saxon *be* which means "by" and *lief* which means "life." What one lives by is actually his belief or his *by-life.* This is the Christian meaning of belief and faith.

CLARENCE JORDAN,
The Substance of Faith

100

The whole biblical history is one of God calling individuals and communities of people to a relationship with Himself as the supreme purpose of life. As the Westminster Catechism puts it, "The chief end of man[kind] is to glorify God and to enjoy him forever." This process is a progressive one, beginning in primitive understandings of God but enlarging and deepening as the history unfolds. Thus we are all involved together in an evolutionary process, and within that process each of us as individuals is called to our own growth and development. The Bible is a manual intended to help us discover the true purpose of life and to grow in our attainment of it.

Jesus announced, "I have come that they may have life, and have it to the full" (John 10:10). And in John, chapter 17, he prayed, "Now this is eternal life: that they may know you, the only true God, and Jesus Christ, whom you have sent. . . . that all of them may be one, Father, just as you are in me and I am in you. . . . I in them and you in me." Thus the ultimate purpose of life is declared to be union with God, as other great religions also propose.

Paul the apostle declared his life's purpose when he said, "I want to know Christ and the power of his resurrection and the fellowship of sharing in his sufferings, becoming like him in his death, and so, somehow, to attain to the resurrection from the dead" (Philippians 3:10,11).

And its power: "I have been crucified with Christ and I no longer live, but Christ lives in me. The life I now live in the body, I live by faith in the Son of God who loved me and gave himself for me" (Galatians 2:20).

And the process is described by Peter: "Grace and peace be yours in abundance through the knowledge of God and of Jesus our Lord. His divine power has given us everything we need for life and godliness through our knowledge of him who called us by his own glory and goodness. Through these he has given us his very great and precious promises, so that through them you may participate in the divine nature. . . . For this reason, make every effort to add to your faith goodness; and to goodness, knowledge; and to knowledge, self-control; and to self-control, perseverance; and to perseverance, godliness; and to godliness, brotherly kindness; and to brotherly kindness, love. . . . Therefore, my brothers, be all the more eager to make your calling and election sure. For if you do these things, you will never fall" (II Peter 1:2–10).

The vision of the psychotherapeutic journey is clearly limited to the enlightenment of one's self *to* one's self. The focus is on the psyche. The spiritual journey, on the other hand, envisions transcending one's self and becoming open to and one with God or the Mystery of the cosmos. For Christians at least, the focus is on God.

Stated this way, it looks like psychology and spirituality are two legs of the same journey. You would seem to begin on the psychological path and then continue along the spiritual path.

But there happens to be a paradox involved in the interface between psychology and spirituality that makes things more complicated. Oddly enough, the psychological portion of the journey seems to focus on strengthening the ego, whereas the spiritual part clearly envisions giving it up. . . .

Psychospiritual growth is a process of gaining control and giving it up, of acquiring ego strength and then surrendering it. Sometimes it is a dramatic flip, as when a sociopath (all ego) turns saint (all God) (Paul on the road to Damascus?). More often, the journey entails an upward back-and-forth rhythm in which each increment of self is first affirmed, then transformed into God. . . .

Visualized like this, spirituality and psychology seem more like integrally connected, parallel aspects of the same journey. A visual aid that's been useful to me in understanding "how it looks" is a double helix, rather like a DNA molecule. One strand of the double spiral represents the psychological or ego dimension; the other strand, the spiritual dimension. Like the DNA molecule, there are a series of links between the two strands. Also like the DNA molecule, the strands are twisted; it's a tortuous journey.

There is at least one drawback in this visual analogy. Unlike DNA, the two strands of the psychospiritual journey are not equal in either strength or intensity. The dominant strand is the spiritual one. The journey's progress is initiated on the psychic strand as some chunk of the ego is affirmed, and then achieves fruition by jumping across one of the links to the spiritual strand, as that chunk of ego is transcended. The directionality, then, aside from the upward progression along the double helix, is always *from* the psychic strand *to* the spiritual strand.

Is doing the work involved in the psychological dimension—acquiring a sense of autonomy and self-determination—a prerequisite for spiritual growth? I think it is. I'm convinced of the wisdom of those spiritual masters who contend that "you have to have an ego before you can give it up."

JOHN FORTUNATO,
Embracing the Exile

The Miracle of Grace

Looking Back

In the last session you sought to define spiritual growth, to evaluate where you are on your own spiritual journey and to specify what are your basic beliefs, acknowledging the fact that everyone has a world view or a religion. What happened to you and others in the meetings? What discomfort or longing did you carry away from the meeting? Take a few minutes to record your feelings and wants in the space below:

_____

_____

_____

_____

_____

_____

_____

_____

_____

_____

_____

_____

_____

Looking Ahead

Read pages 235–71 in *The Road Less Traveled* on Grace and the four miracles Scott Peck says he has encountered in his therapeutic practice and which he sees as empirical evidence of a loving God. Only when you have read the text, go on to the preparatory exercises that follow:

1. Your assignment last week was to look for miracles each day, so you've been getting some good practice. Peck says, on page 238, "There is a force, the mechanics of which we do not fully understand, that seems to operate routinely in most people to protect and to foster their mental health even under the most adverse conditions." On page 240 he enlarges this statement to include physical health. Take a few minutes to review your life history. What health hazards have you resisted and survived? Where are you most aware of the miracle of your health? _____

_____

_____

_____

_____

_____

2. Peck says, "There is a part of us that is wiser than we are. . . . To educate is 'to bring out of,' 'to lead forth.' " He lists dreams, idle thoughts, slips of the tongue and "mistakes" as sources of insight breaking through from unconsciousness to awareness. How do you usually deal with these "sources of wisdom"? ____

_____

_____

_____

_____

3. When have you taken one seriously, and what did you learn?

_____

_____

_____

_____

4. Peck says, "A major and essential task in the process of one's spiritual development is the continuous work of bringing one's conscious self-concept into progressively greater congruence with reality." We are faced with the problem of how to stop hiding our reality from ourselves. How do you see yourself working on this major task in your life? Or resisting working on it? _____

_____

_____

_____

_____

_____

5. Grace: "a powerful force originating outside of human consciousness which nurtures the spiritual growth of human
   beings." When have you felt Grace at work in your life? _____

_____

_____

_____

_____

6. Complete, in your own words, Peck's statement: "The idea that
   God is actively nurturing us so that we might grow up to be like
   Him/Her" brings me face to face with _____

_____

_____

_____

_____

_____

Resources for the Road

*The most beautiful and profound emotion we can experience
is the sensation of the mystical. It is the sower of all science.
[The one] to whom this emotion is a stranger, who can no longer
wonder and stand rapt in awe, is as good as dead. To know
what is impenetrable to us really exists, manifesting itself as the*

highest wisdom and the most radiant beauty which our dull faculties can comprehend only in their most primitive forms— this knowledge, this feeling is at the center of religiousness.

> ALBERT EINSTEIN,
> quoted by Lincoln Barnett in
> *The Universe and Dr. Einstein*

Eyes must be opened to inner reality. Such an "opening of one's eyes," a revelation, can never be given directly in so many words. We see inner reality only through an "aha!" experience, a sudden insight into our own being. There is no way to describe inner reality directly.

> JOHN SANFORD,
> *The Kingdom Within*

Knowledge seems more like a kind of pain-killing drug that I have to take repeatedly against the burden and desolation of my heart. And no matter how faithful I may be to it, it can never really cure me. All it can give me is words and concepts which perform the middleman's service of expressing and interpreting reality to me, but can never still my heart's craving for the reality itself, for true life and true possession. I shall never be cured until all reality comes streaming like an ecstatic intoxicating melody into my heart.

> KARL RAHNER

Suddenly. The encrustations of sophistication fall away and we find ourselves standing in front of the bare fact of being.

One day, perhaps, you are watching an ordinary ladybug climb up an old beige curtain with sun-faded forget-me-nots still blooming in the background pattern. Suddenly, the bug crosses the invisible line between being an assumed part of the known world, with a name and a classification, and becomes a marvel. You find yourself wondering why there are ladybugs. And what would it be like to be a ladybug? And does it look at me and wonder?

Willi Unsoeld, who was on the American team that first climbed Mt. Everest, told me that when he was returning from the peak, he paused on a high col to admire the view. Turning around, he saw a small blue flower in the snow. "I don't know how to describe what happened," he said. "Everything opened up and flowed together and made some strange kind of sense. And I was at complete peace. I have no idea how long I stood there. It could have been minutes or hours. Time melted. But when I came down, my life was different. . . ."

It can happen anywhere, anytime. The shock of wonder is an earthquake that changes our perception of ourselves and the world and rearranges the foundations of our identity. A tidal wave of astonishment washes away the polite virtues of the adult, the self-sufficiency of the outlaw. Explanations, myths, ideologies crumble like so many sand castles. When the shock recedes, we are left with a memory of having been in the presence of the holy, the awesome and fascinating mystery (*mysterium: tremendum et fascinans*—as Rudolph Otto called it).

SAM KEEN,
The Passionate Life

Statistically, the probability of any one of us being here is so small that you'd think the mere fact of existing would keep us all in a contented dazzlement of surprise. We are alive against the stupendous odds of genetics, infinitely outnumbered by all the alternatives who might, except for luck, be in our places.

. . .

We violate probability, by our nature. To be able to do this systematically, and in such wild varieties of form, from viruses to whales, is extremely unlikely; to have sustained the effort successfully for several billion years of our existence, without drifting back into randomness, was nearly a mathematical impossibility.

Add to this the biological improbability that makes each member of our own species unique. Everyone is one in 3 billion at the moment, which describes the odds. Each of us is a self-contained, free-standing individual, labeled by specific protein configurations at the surfaces of cells, identifiable by whorls of fingertip skin, maybe even by special medleys of fragrance. You'd think we'd never stop dancing.

LEWIS THOMAS, M.D.,
Lives of a Cell

The real amazement, if you want to be amazed, is the process [of conception]. You start out as a single cell derived from the coupling of a sperm and an egg, this divides into two, then four, then eight, and so on, and at a certain stage there emerges a single cell which will have as all its progeny the human brain. The mere existence of that cell should be one of the great astonishments of the earth. People ought to be walking around all day, all through their waking hours, calling to each other in endless wonderment, talking of nothing except that cell. It is an unbelievable thing, and yet there it is, popping neatly into its place amid the jumbled cells of every one of the several billion human embryos around the planet, just as if it were the easiest thing in the world to do.

If you like being surprised, there's the source. One cell is switched on to become the whole trillion-cell, massive apparatus for thinking and imagining, and, for that matter, for being surprised. All the information needed for learning to read and write, playing the piano, arguing before senatorial sub-committees, walking across a street through traffic, or the marvelous human act of putting out one hand and leaning against a tree, is contained in that first cell. All of grammar, all syntax, all arithmetic, all music. . . .

No one has the ghost of an idea how this works, and nothing else in life can ever be so puzzling. If anyone does succeed in explaining it, within my lifetime, I will charter a skywriting airplane, maybe a whole fleet of them, and send them aloft to write one great exclamation point after another, around the whole sky, until all my money runs out.

> LEWIS THOMAS, M.D.,
> *The Medusa and the Snail*

Besides all this, biblical faith claims that within a process in history, recorded in the Old and New Testaments, the Creator has been uniquely revealed through a serious of gracious actions.

Beginning with the choice of Abraham and his descendants, with whom God entered into covenant relationship—"not because you were more in number than any other people . . . but because the Lord loved you" (Deuteronomy 7:7)—and throughout Israel's long history, God has acted in grace.

112

The greatest single action in Israel's history, to which the psalms and the prophets repeatedly hark back, is their miraculous deliverance from slavery in Egypt and their safe conduct through the wilderness to the land of promise. (See Deuteronomy 7:18,19; Psalms 78, 106.)

Christian faith sees the culmination of this process of revelation in the "incarnation" of God in human life—in the birth, death and resurrection of Jesus of Nazareth. To this day, the remembrance of these events in the sharing of bread and wine—"This do in remembrance of me"—is the central ritual of Christian faith, a constant reminder of God's grace, a recognition that in response to faith God offers forgiveness, redemption and transformation of life.

Thus John 1:14, 17 declare: "The Word was made flesh and dwelt among us, full of grace and truth. . . . Grace and truth came by Jesus Christ."

Paul declares, in Romans 3:24, "[All] are justified freely by this grace through the redemption that came by Jesus Christ." "Therefore, since we have been justified through faith, we have peace with God through our Lord Jesus Christ, through whom we have gained access by faith into this grace in which we now stand" (Romans 5:1,2).

Resisting and Welcoming Grace

Looking Back

In your last group session you pondered the reality of four miracles, health, the unconscious, serendipities and evolution, which Scott Peck sees as evidences of the existence of Grace. What happened in the meeting and what do you want to record of your feelings and wishes?

_____

_____

_____

_____

_____

_____

_____

_____

_____

_____

_____

_____

_____

Looking Ahead

Before reading the final section of *The Road Less Traveled*, place yourself where you feel you belong on this continuum:

MY RESPONSE TO GRACE

I want none of it   I am open to all of it

Why did you choose to place yourself there? _____

_____

_____

_____

Now read pages 271–312 and after finishing your reading make a brief inventory of your life under these two headings:

WAYS I RESIST GRACE	WAYS I OPEN MYSELF TO GRACE

Peck postulates that Grace originates in a God who is "intimately associated with us—so intimately that He is part of us" (p. 281). And, "We are born that we might become, as a conscious individual, a new life form of God" (p. 283). What are your gut responses to this viewpoint? Write down your feelings, rapidly, not in sentences or with any premeditation. Keep writing until you must stop. _____

_____

_____

_____

_____

"Grace brings its dark, frightening face as well as its glory," Peck says. What can you recall as the frightening aspects of Grace? Of its glory? _____

_____

_____

_____

_____

This "source of agony" becomes in our lives a source of power and wisdom by which problems become _____

Barriers become _____

Unwanted thoughts become_____

Feelings become _____

Symptoms become _____
(See p. 296.)

117

Imagine that you have a friend who has struggled with mental illness. Write a brief letter explaining to him or her Peck's insights about Grace and mental illness. _____

_____

_____

_____

_____

_____

_____

Peck says, "We live our lives in the eye of God, and not at the periphery but at the center of His vision, His concern. It is probable that the universe as we know it is but a single stepping-stone toward the entrance to the Kingdom of God" (p. 312). Through the ages people like you have expressed to God their feelings in response to grace, both their fear-resistance and joy-welcome. As your final exercise, write a letter, poem, prayer, or psalm addressed to the Giver of Grace. _____

_____

_____

_____

_____

_____

_____

_____

_____

Look back now at the first exercise and see if you wish to relocate yourself on the continuum. If so, what changes do you see in your relationship to the Giver of Grace? _____

_____

_____

_____

Resources for the Road

If your daily life seems poor, do not blame it; blame yourself, tell yourself that you are not poet enough to call forth its riches; for to the creator there is no poverty and no poor indifferent place. . . . For the creator must be a world for himself and find everything in himself and in nature to whom he has attached himself.

RAINER MARIA RILKE,
Letters to a Young Poet

If we do not believe, the waves engulf us,
the winds blow, nourishment fails,
sickness lays us low or kills us,
the divine power is impotent or remote,
If, on the other hand, we believe,
the waters are welcoming and sweet,
the bread is multiplied, our eyes are open,
the dead rise again,
the power of God is as it were
drawn from him by force
and spreads throughout all nature.

PIERRE TEILHARD DE CHARDIN

Faith involves a belief in God that arouses us to action, that fills us with a lived conviction that the universe is permeated with a redeeming love. God did not create men and women as automated robots or helpless puppets, but enabled them somehow to shape their own destiny within the innumerable possibilities created by his divine love. Such a faith gives meaning to human love—and to life itself.

THOMAS J. O'CONNOR

Do you know what it means to be struck by grace? . . . We cannot transform our lives, unless we allow them to be transformed by that stroke of grace. It happens; or it does not happen. And certainly it does *not* happen if we try to force it upon ourselves, just as it shall not happen so long as we think, in our self-complacency, that we have no need of it. Grace strikes us when we are in great pain and restlessness. It strikes us when we walk through the dark valley of a meaningless and empty life. It strikes us when we feel that our separation is deeper than usual, because we have violated another life, a life which we loved, or from which we were estranged. It strikes us when our disgust for our own being, our indifference, our weakness, our hostility, and our lack of direction and composure have become intolerable to us. It strikes us when, year after year, the longed-for perfection of life does not appear, when the old compulsions reign within us as they have for decades, when despair destroys all joy and courage.

Sometimes at that moment a wave of light breaks into our darkness, and it is as though a voice were saying: "You are accepted. *You are accepted,* accepted by that

120

which is greater than you, and the name of which you do not know. Do not ask for the name now; perhaps you will find it later. Do not try to do anything now; perhaps later you will do much. Do not seek for anything; do not perform anything; do not intend anything. *Simply accept the fact that you are accepted!*" If that happens to us, we experience grace. After such an experience we may not be better than before, and we may not believe more than before. But everything is transformed. In that moment, grace conquers sin, and reconciliation bridges the gulf of estrangement. And nothing is demanded of this experience, no religious or moral or intellectual presupposition, nothing but *acceptance.* . . .

It is such moments that make us love our life, that make us accept ourselves, not in our goodness and self-complacency, but in our certainty of the eternal meaning of our life. We cannot force ourselves to accept ourselves. We cannot compel anyone to accept himself. But sometimes it happens that we receive the power to say "yes" to ourselves, that peace enters into us and makes us whole, that self-hate and self-contempt disappear, and that our self is reunited with itself. Then we can say that grace has come upon us.

> PAUL TILLICH,
> *The Shaking of the Foundations*

Late have I loved you, O Beauty ever ancient, ever new!
Late have I loved you! and behold
You were within, and I without,
  and without I sought You.
And deformed I ran after those forms of beauty You have made.
You were with me and I was not with You.

Those things held me back from You,
  things whose only being was to be in You.
You called; You cried;
  and You broke through my deafness.
You flashed; You shone;
  and You chased away my blindness.
You became fragrant;
  and I inhaled and sighed for You.
I tasted,
  and now hunger and thirst for You.
You touched me;
  and I burned for Your embrace.

St. Augustine,
Confessions

Both Jewish and Christian Scriptures echo Peck's statement, on page 300, that "most of us choose not to heed the call of grace and reject its assistance."

When the Israelites approached the Promised Land and sent twelve spies ahead to reconnoiter, only two encouraged them to go forward. The whole community voted not to risk the undertaking and that entire generation was condemned to wander in the wilderness and die before their descendants were permitted to occupy the land. (See Numbers, chapters 13,14.)

A recurring theme throughout the prophetic writings is that though the nation may suffer or perish in disobedience there will always be a "remnant" who remain faithful. (See Isaiah 1:9; 37:32; 46:3; Micah 2:12.)

In the New Testament, the apostle Paul reviews Israel's history and concludes, "Now these things occurred as examples, to keep us from setting our hearts on evil things as they did . . . and were written down as warnings for us" (I Corinthians 10:1–11).

Throughout the Letter to the Hebrews there are repeated warnings such as this: "The Holy Spirit says . . . 'Do not harden your hearts as you did in the rebellion, during the time of testing in the desert, where your fathers tested and tried me.' . . . See to it, brothers, that none of you has a sinful, unbelieving heart that turns away from the living God" (Hebrews 3:7–12).

Peck quotes Jesus' statement, "Many are called, but few are chosen" (Matthew 22:14). Jesus also said, "Enter through the narrow gate. For wide is the gate and broad is the road that leads to destruction, and many enter through it. But small is the gate and narrow the road that leads to life, and only a few find it" (Matthew 7:13,14).

But strong as are the warnings, the welcome of Grace calls out even more strongly.

"Come, all you who are thirsty," God says through the prophet Isaiah, "come to the waters; and you who have no money, come, buy and eat! . . . Give ear and come to me; hear me, that your soul may live. . . . Turn to the Lord and he will have mercy, and to our God, for he will freely pardon" (Isaiah 55:1–7).

Jesus says, "Come to me, all you who are weary and burdened, and I will give you rest. Take my yoke upon you and learn from me, for I am gentle and humble in heart, and you will find rest for your souls. For my yoke is easy and my burden is light" (Matthew 11:28–30).

And this: "Be earnest and repent. Here I am! I stand at the door and knock. If anyone hears my voice and opens the door, I will come in and eat with him, and he with me" (Revelation 3:20).

> *My children, mark me, I pray you. Know! God loves my soul so much that His very life and being depends upon God's loving me whether He would or not. To stop God from loving me would be to rob Him of His Godhood.*
>
> MEISTER ECKHART

123

The Leader's Guide

What follows are step-by-step procedures for leading a group through the process of interacting with the concepts in *The Road Less Traveled*.

This may be your introduction to an experiential approach to education, where the focus is on *learning*, not *teaching*. The object is to provide a climate that facilitates and supports group members as they struggle with the complex process of growth and change. It is an approach that may be new even to many seasoned professionals, but which is gaining in popularity because it is a more effective approach to learning than most traditional methods.

To be effective you will need to take whatever time and energy is required to immerse yourself in the learning and growing process. You will need to do the exercises in the participants' workbook along with them, and be willing to be stretched and changed by the process. It will take effort and work but the results, for yourself as well as the participants, will far outweigh any sacrifices you make.

WHAT YOU NEED TO GET STARTED

1. Eager and committed participants
2. An optimum-sized group
3. A comfortable, informal meeting place

---

1. PARTICIPANTS Look for men and women who want to grow, who are willing to give the course high priority and are able to invest the time and energy required.

2. SIZE Between eight and sixteen seems optimum, enough for stimulating diversity of experience and viewpoints, but not enough to make participation unwieldy.

3. MEETING PLACE Choose an informal setting with movable chairs and adequate space for spreading out, to allow both for "alone time" and for dividing into smaller groupings, as the exercises may call for.

Every group needs clearly delineated norms that are agreed upon and kept visible at every session. We suggest you put the following on newsprint and obtain group consensus that they are to govern your interactions in each meeting of the group.

GROUP NORMS

1. Take responsibility for your own learning.
2. Be regular and on time.
3. When you speak, speak only for yourself. Use "I" messages.
4. When others speak, listen caringly,
   without judging or evaluating.
5. Give everyone the opportunity to participate equally.
6. Respect confidentiality; nothing personal goes outside the group.

You may wish to share the leadership of the group, especially if you know someone else who is qualified and wishes to be involved. There are advantages in such sharing. It enables you to alternate leadership tasks so that while one is leading the other can observe. You can participate in the exercises, filling in when needed to provide the right number for smaller groupings. There is great value in giving yourself to the process and sharing yourself as openly as you ask your group members to do. Sharing leadership also enables you to assess the meeting afterward, to give and get feedback and improve your leadership style.

We have always worked as a team and find it a distinct advantage. One of us is better at giving instructions and seeing that the process moves along on time, while the other is better at reading the feelings of participants and sensing what may be going on between them. Both skills are valuable and it is a gift when shared leadership brings these complementary gifts into play.

The exercises we have designed for each of the twelve sessions that follow are of two kinds. Some refer back to the participants' workbook and the expectation is that participants will complete their assignments and bring the results to the group session. If they have not done so, they can still participate in the group exercise but may not benefit from it as much as if they had prepared for it beforehand.

Other exercises will be new to the participants. In some cases their value will depend on the surprise element with which they are introduced or the spontaneity they call for. Participants should be asked, therefore, not to look ahead in the leader's material but to concentrate on reading the assigned pages in *The Road Less Traveled* and doing the exercises given them in their workbook.

Here are some general guidelines for your direction of the process, once your group gets started:

1. BRIDGING Your instructions will usually allow some time to report on what has been happening since the last session, and an opportunity to relax and become "present" for the session about to begin. Be sensitive to the energy level as you start each meeting. Remember, participants are coming from a variety of situations, some stressful and demanding, and they need a chance to have their feelings and concerns recognized before they can lay them aside and be ready for what is about to claim their attention.

2. ABSENCES Recognize and explain any necessary absences that have been reported in. This assumes that group members are to call you when they must be absent or late.

3. AGENDA Display a statement of purpose and a time schedule at the start of each group session, so that participants can anticipate when they enter the room how the time will be spent.

4. TIMING Sometimes an exercise will need more time than is allotted, or the group may wish to spend more time on a particular issue than the design calls for. Allow yourself a certain amount of flexibility. Good timing is the ability to strike a balance between the structure of your design, with its goals, and the needs of your

group, which are unpredictable and constantly changing. A good leader constantly keeps one eye on the clock while keeping touch with the pulse of the group, so that the session moves toward its goal by fulfilling the needs of the participants and not at their expense.

5. AFFIRMATION Some of the exercises are rigorous and demanding. Be sure to thank your group when they function well. Some call for the revealing of intimate feelings and very personal experiences, which may be difficult and even unsettling for a few. Affirmation is an important reward for taking risks. If your group has worked hard and intently, be sure to encourage self-affirmation.

6. CLOSING The instructions that follow suggest procedures for closing each session but you may wish to adapt them as you sense how comfortable or uncomfortable your group is with touching. We feel that physical contact is important for a group to reinforce the belonging and support that is essential to its effectiveness. Hopefully your group will soon feel comfortable forming a circle (holding hands or placing arms around each others' shoulders) as you part. You may wish to hold up personal concerns that can be remembered during the time between sessions. Some groups will feel comfortable praying, either aloud or silently. Though the focus of these sessions is personal learning it is inevitable that closeness and caring will develop as you become a group. That's an added dividend that comes with exploring with others *The Road Less Traveled*.

SESSION ONE: *Life Is Difficult*

GOALS OF THIS SESSION: (1) To become acquainted; (2) to express personal expectations for the course; (3) to clarify procedures that will be followed; (4) to give an overview of the subject matter to be covered; and (5) to interact with the introductory theme that life is difficult because it is meant for learning and growing. (Put as much of this as seems appropriate on newsprint and display it before the group.)

MATERIALS NEEDED: Sheets of 8½-by-11-inch paper, magic markers, string, pins or masking tape, pens or pencils, notebooks or journals (to be furnished by participants).

GETTING STARTED: (5 minutes) As people enter the room, have them make name tags and begin to get acquainted with each other. Refreshments may be made available, although we recommend that they be served instead at a break time midway through the session.

Exercise 1: The Difficult/Easy Continuum (20 minutes)

Place a sign on one wall reading, "VERY DIFFICULT," on the facing wall another sign reading, "VERY EASY," and place a string on the floor running from one wall to the other. Ask participants to place themselves on the line at the point between the two extremes that represents how they see their own lives now in terms of difficulty and ease. *This is to be done in silence* and, when everyone has taken a position, take a moment to notice together where people have positioned themselves. Have each participant choose a partner next to them on the line, move away and talk for five minutes about the reason for their positioning and their feelings about what they have done. At the end of the time bring the entire group back together and give an opportunity to share whatever learnings came through the experience.

Rationale for the course: (15 minutes)

Spend a few minutes reviewing the material in the introduction to the participants' guide (beginning on page 127) so that everyone has a clear understanding of the norms by which your group will function (the need to be prompt, to report necessary absences ahead of time, to open oneself to the exercises in order to maximize personal learning, to respect confidentiality and so on). Display them on newsprint. Share your own enthusiasm for the book and what you hope to see accomplished in the next twelve weeks.

(OPTIONAL: Pass around a sheet of paper on which each person is to write name, address and telephone number so that at the next session a group roster can be made available.)

Be sure that each participant has a copy of *The Road Less Traveled*, and review briefly Scott Peck's opening statements on pages 15–18: "Life is difficult. . . . Life is a series of problems. . . . We attempt to skirt around problems rather than meet them head on. . . . This tendency to avoid problems and the emotional suffering inherent in them is the primary basis of all human mental illness."

Exercise 2: How We Avoid Problems (30 minutes)

Give participants sheets of paper and magic markers. Have them write in print large enough to read three feet away the ways in which they customarily avoid problems. Before they begin let one of the enablers "model" by sharing at least the beginnings of the list. (In our first group one of us wrote the following:)

```
HOPE THEY'LL GO AWAY
WATCH TV
BLAME OTHER PEOPLE
WAIT FOR SOMEONE/SOMETHING
TO SOLVE THEM FOR ME
```

When everyone has written a list, have them stand up, hold them in front of them, mill around in silence (with no talking) and read what others have written. After sufficient time, divide into triads (choosing two people with whom you have much in common), sit down facing each other and share your feelings about your avoiding behavior.

Bathroom and refreshments break: (10 minutes)

Exercise 3: Learning from Problems (35 minutes)

Model from your own experience of growing through problems by describing briefly an experience that was difficult at the time but that turned out to be a learning situation through which personal growth was enhanced. Here is an example from an actual session:

"During an unwanted separation I was continually faced with the problem and pain of living alone. For months I resisted; I found ways to avoid it; I refused to face the fact that I *was* alone. I spent so much wasted time fighting it, blaming others for it, and generally ignoring an opportunity to learn from my pain—to see that I was stronger than I thought, that I could live on my own, secure in who I was. It took a long time before I stopped fighting and faced my problems. Then I began to learn. For sure, I needed to recover from my shock first, but I now see that I could have begun learning sooner had I faced my problem rather than run from it."

Give each participant paper and pen and ask them to write for ten minutes on a recent situation in which they encountered a difficulty. Did they face it? If so, how, and what did they learn from it? If not, what opportunity for learning might they have missed? What might they still do about it? What *will* they do?

In the total group ask individuals who may care to do so to report whatever learnings came to them in the process of writing (journaling). Do not force participants to share but allow them the opportunity to do so.

ALTERNATIVE TO EXERCISES 2 AND 3: You may wish, instead, to spend this time getting better acquainted, thus building a deeper sense of group solidarity. Ask participants to share something of the "road" or journey they have traveled up to now—whatever they wish the group to know about them, including some of the things they have found easy and difficult along the way. Let one of the leaders begin the sharing, modeling as you do so the kinds of things that will be helpful to others to know about you—who you are, how you have experienced life, and how you have come to the place where you are now on the road. Agree on a specific time for each person and stick to it.

CLOSURE: One appropriate way to close your meeting might be to form a circle and have someone read the poignant words of Kahlil Gibran on "Pain" that follow, or it can be duplicated for each member to read aloud together.

Pain

And a woman spoke, saying, "Tell us of pain."
And he said,

Your pain is the breaking of the shell that encloses your
understanding.

Even as the stone of the fruit must break, that its heart
may stand in the sun, so must you know pain.

And could you keep your heart in wonder at the daily
miracles of your life, your pain would not seem less
wondrous than your joy;

And you would accept the seasons of your heart; even as
you have always accepted the seasons that pass over
your field.

And you would watch with serenity through the winters
of your grief.

Much of your pain is self chosen.

It is the bitter potion by which the physician within you
heals your sick self.

Therefore trust the physician, and drink his remedy in
silence and tranquillity;

For his hand, though heavy and hard, is guided by the
tender hand of the Unseen,

And the cup he brings, though it burn your lips, has
been fashioned of the clay which the Potter has
moistened with His own sacred tears.

KAHLIL GIBRAN,
The Prophet

ASSIGNMENT: Read pages 1–32 in *The Road Less Traveled,* paying
special attention to pages 18–20, which describe the first tool for
solving problems: "Delaying Gratification," and do the exercises in
Lesson 1 of the participants' workbook, beginning on page 17.

SESSION TWO: *Delaying Gratification*
Pages 1–32 in *The Road Less Traveled*

GOAL OF THIS SESSION: To confront our patterns of satisfying and delaying gratification.

MATERIALS NEEDED: Newsprint, felt-tip pens, record player and record for background of quiet instrumental music, paper and pencils or pens.

SUMMARY OF CONTENT: Scott Peck defines delaying gratification as "a process of scheduling the pain and pleasure of life in such a way as to enhance the pleasure by meeting and experiencing the pain first and getting it over with." Too often we avoid problems hoping they will go away of their own accord. Our capacity to delay gratification depends on having "self-disciplined role models, a sense of self-worth, and a degree of trust in the safety of our existence."

GETTING STARTED: (10 minutes) Take a moment or two to see how people are feeling and whether there are concerns they need to voice and then set aside in order to be fully present to the process of the session. Allow a few minutes for feedback on the questions participants were to be asking themselves during the past week. Share any discoveries that seem important enough to report before you move into the new material.

Exercise 1: *Delaying and Gratifying Touch* (20 minutes)

Announce that you as a group will be working hard in this session but will begin with a few minutes of play. Divide into triads, with leaders participating or sitting out as needed to insure a multiple of three. Let them decide who will go first, second and third, and then explain what they will be doing.

Whoever begins will stand bending over, with head down and arms hanging loosely while the other two, standing on each side facing each other, tap the first person's neck, shoulders, and arms, using simultaneous motions (such as vigorous tapping, using finger-tips or the sides of one's hands, or both alternately) for about two minutes while the other person simply receives. Do this in silence.

After two minutes, call time and rotate, so that person number two receives. Then announce that this is all the time you can give to this. You're sorry to have to leave anyone out. And then, (after the uproar has subsided), ask such questions as, "What feelings did you experience? How did you decide who would go first, second, third? What does this mirror of your normal behavior?" Once you've completed this, allow the third person to be tapped, so that no one is actually deprived of this enjoyable experience.

CLARIFYING THE ISSUES: (5 minutes) Use this experience as a spring-board for drawing from the group a discussion of delaying gratifi-cation. How does Peck define it? What does it have to do with procrastination, impulsiveness, problem solving? Does delaying gratification have value in itself or is it the *ability* to delay, when one needs to, that is of value? What three factors condition us from childhood to be able to discipline ourselves? (See p. 26 in *The Road Less Traveled*.)

Exercise 2: Childhood Messages (30 minutes)

In the same groups of three, share memories of how your basic needs were met as a child and what your experiences were of delaying gratification. What was modeled by your parents? What did they teach you verbally? Participants who have prepared for the session will be able to share from their workbooks, pages 19–20.

Before engaging in the exercise itself, model briefly out of your own experience to set the tone of the sharing which is hoped for. For example, in one group, the following was shared:

"My parents modeled a very disciplined style of living. Duty was a high value that they impressed on me. Both of them worked and were extremely busy. Saturday afternoons were reserved for family adventures, like hikes and picnics. We could not study on Sunday, so I learned to do it before that. Work always had to be done (homework and chores) before I was entitled to play. I chafed under this, but today I am fairly well able to discipline my desires. Yet I have this strong impulse at times to forget my duties and indulge in 'meaningless' play."

After 20 minutes call the entire group together and let them report whatever learnings seem appropriate to share with others. In our group a distinction was drawn between *delaying* and *denying* gratification. Some reported that they had been denied certain gratifications out of necessity (their families were poor or remotely situated) while others were denied for religious reasons. The latter reason gave rise to expressions of still lingering resentment.

A distinction was also made between various sorts of gratifications (physical, economic, emotional, spiritual, for example) and the things that promise gratification but do not deliver. Short-term gratification was contrasted with long-term gratification.

BREAK: (10 minutes)

Exercise 3: Cultural Forces (15 minutes)

Brainstorm some of the cultural forces we feel today, either encouraging delay of gratification or discouraging it. Participants who

137

have prepared will be reporting from their workbooks, pages 20–21. Put what is said on newsprint so all can see it. Don't evaluate, judge or debate the input, but when reporting is completed allow participants to report what force(s) have the most power in their lives.

Here is an example of what one group produced. What will your group come up with?

FORCES FOR DELAYING	FORCES AGAINST
Need for education	Credit cards/charge accounts
Recession	Advertising commercials
My faith	New sexual mores
Psychotherapy	Self-fulfillment pop psychology
Goals and aspirations	Enslavement to feelings
Fidelity to a commitment	

Exercise 4: Scheduling the Pain (25 minutes)

With soft instrumental music (without words) playing in the background, invite each participant to sit comfortably (or lie on the floor) and reflect for five minutes on how the discipline of delaying gratification has been helpful. When has it helped you solve problems and grow, and when has the failure to delay gratification complicated problems or left them unsolved?

Bring the reflection time to a close and invite participants to write for ten minutes in their journals on a situation or an aspect of their life where they are having difficulty delaying gratification. What do they want to do about it?

In the remaining time, choose a partner and share what you wish of your intentions. You may want to make yourself accountable to your partner in some way, to report back at some appropriate time what action you have or have not taken.

CLOSURE: You may wish to form a circle, thank the group for their hard work, have everyone make eye contact around the circle and nonverbally express good wishes for the coming week.

ASSIGNMENT: Read pages 32–44 in *The Road Less Traveled* on "Responsibility," and do the exercises in Lesson 2 in the participants' workbook, beginning on page 27.

SESSION THREE: Accepting Responsibility
Pages 32–44 in *The Road Less Traveled*

GOAL OF THIS SESSION: To be aware of our feelings and attitudes as well as our responsibility and to identify changes we wish to make.

MATERIALS NEEDED: Newsprint, felt-tip markers

SUMMARY OF CONTENT: The problem of distinguishing what we are and what we are not responsible for in this life is difficult, but we must assume responsibility for what is properly ours, not blaming others or avoiding the pain of resolving our problems. Psychological disorders are generally "disorders of responsibility." Neurotics assume too much responsibility; those with character disorders, not enough. Most of us do some of both.

GETTING STARTED: (10 minutes) Allow a few minutes for reporting in thoughts, feelings and learnings from the week, particularly those relating to what participants recorded in their workbooks about the last session.

Exercise 1: Blaming and Placating (20 minutes)

Divide into two groups. Stand facing each other, so each person has an "opponent." Let one side take the role of the blamers. Get into the feelings accompanying the act of blaming. What bodily posture is appropriate? What gestures? (Such as looking down their noses, pointing fingers, puffing up chests) What words? What tone of voice? (Loudness, harshness) Let that side rehearse briefly, using such words as "You did it!" "It's all your fault!" "You never listen!" and so on.

Let those facing them become placaters. What bodily posture is appropriate? (Heads down, eyes downcast) What words? What tone of voice? (Muffled murmurs) Let them rehearse briefly, using such words as "I'm sorry," "I didn't mean to," and "You're right; you're right!"

At the signal let both lines act out their parts simultaneously, blamers blaming and placaters placating for two minutes or so. Then switch roles. Let blamers become placaters and placaters become blamers. After two minutes or so, call time, let participants share with the one opposite them their feelings in acting out their roles. What insights or learnings can they derive from the exercise? Share some of these in the total group.

Exercise 2: My Pattern of Responsibility (25 minutes)

Now that you have gotten in touch with some of the feelings that accompany avoiding responsibility (blaming) and assuming too much responsibility (placating), choose a partner (or stay with the same one with whom you have just role-played, if you wish) and sit down facing each other to identify specific situations in your lives that relate to these issues. Decide who is going to begin and let that person, for two minutes, state and keep repeating the statement, "Something I avoid responsibility for is . . .," each time citing another specific example, while the other person simply listens in silence. (Let the leader(s) model briefly what is expected.) After two minutes, switch roles while the first person listens in silence for two minutes and the second person makes a series of statements.

For the next step, let the first person repeat the statement, "Something I take *too much* responsibility for is . . ." for two minutes. Switch roles for another two minutes. Then encourage partners to share with each other feelings that this exercise aroused and any personal discoveries it led to.

Come back as a total group to share feelings and learnings. Discuss the topic of avoiding responsibility (how we do it and why) or of assuming inappropriate responsibility. Close this portion of the meeting by displaying on newsprint Reinhold Niebuhr's great prayer:

> "God, grant me the serenity to accept the things I cannot change, courage to change the things I can, and wisdom to know the difference."

One of the leaders might wish to model from experience what that prayer has meant in shaping his or her personal behavior.

BREAK: (10 minutes)

Exercise 3: Knowing the Difference (15 minutes)

Brainstorm as a total group ways to determine what is and what is not your own personal responsibility, relating the exercise back to the Serenity Prayer referred to just before the break. Put all ideas on newsprint where everyone can see them. Remember, there is to be no criticizing, evaluating or even discussing ideas at this point. After the list is complete, you might want to prioritize the input, singling out the most helpful suggestions and allowing people to elaborate on how they actually practice them. Be as specific as possible, avoiding broad generalities.

Some of the factors suggested in one session were:

> Distinguish "I can't" from "I won't" and "I don't want to."
> I ask myself, "How am I causing this problem?"
> I ask, "What am I most afraid of?" and do something about it.
> Being aware of what my body is saying.
> Ask, "Is it *my* problem, *your* problem, or *our* problem?"
> Check out my conclusions with trusted friends.

Exercise 4: Analyzing a Problem (25 minutes)

In silence ask each participant to select a specific, real problem he or she is facing and reflect on it, dealing with such questions as, "What aspects of this are my responsibility?" and "What can I do to meet my responsibility in this situation?" Use journal or note-book to record reflections and conclusions.

After 10 or 15 minutes go back to your partner in Exercise 2, describe the problem briefly, your part in it and the action you intend to take to assume responsibility for it. Ask each other questions, if you wish, to clarify issues, but do not give advice unless specifically asked for it. If you wish, make yourselves accountable to each other to check back later on how well you have fulfilled your intentions.

TYING IT ALL TOGETHER: (10 minutes) Draw from the total group whatever learnings have come from this session. Display them on newsprint if you wish.

CLOSURE: Stand in a circle and encourage group members to express their newly chosen goals for accepting responsibility, then repeat together the Serenity Prayer as a way of reinforcing the session's goal.

ASSIGNMENT: Read pages 44–63 in *The Road Less Traveled* on "Dedication to Reality," and do the exercises beginning on page 37.

SESSION FOUR: Dedication to Reality
Pages 44–63 in *The Road Less Traveled*

GOAL OF THIS SESSION: To examine our relationships to reality, both the outer world and our own inner world, and decide where we may want to update them.

MATERIALS NEEDED: Newsprint, felt-tip marker, writing paper, pens or pencils, construction paper, crayons, masking tape, scissors.

SUMMARY OF CONTENT: Our views of reality are like maps with which to negotiate our journey across the terrain of life. If our maps are inaccurate, we will lose our way. So we need constantly to revise them. Though that may prove a difficult and painful process, it enables us to become better oriented to our present world.

Clinging to outmoded maps may lead to mental illness. Psychotherapy is, in part, a process of map revising which must begin with stringent examination of our ways of seeing reality, sometimes a process more painful than examining the world around us.

Dedication to truth means not only new ways of seeing but also a willingness to change, which must become a way of life. Growing people are "open" people. Total honesty does not mean, however, that there are not times when it is best to withhold some of the truth from others, but the decision to do so must always be based on the real needs of the person from whom it is being withheld, and that decision can be an extremely difficult one to make.

GETTING STARTED: (10 minutes) Allow a few minutes for participants to "settle in" by expressing any feelings they need to "get off their chests," and to share whatever they want to from their workbooks reflecting on the past session. Go over the goals for this session and lead into the first exercise by quoting paragraph one of the summary of content.

Exercise 1: Our Changing Maps (45 minutes)

Give each participant several sheets of white paper and the choice of a few crayons of different colors. Invite them to sit comfortably and silently, closing their eyes, while they let come into their awareness the world as they saw and understood it around the age of eight. Was it closed in or open? Restrictive or freeing? Scary or safe? Uncertain or predictable? After a few minutes, have them draw a representation of their map of their world at that age.

Now recall a time when your world changed. When did it happen, and why? Did you leave home, enter the world of work, were you ill or disappointed by a broken relationship? What was happening in the world at that time? A war, a depression, a time of rapid social change? How did your map of reality change? Make revisions on your eight-year-old map or draw a new map.

If you wish to, draw a third map to represent how you see the

144

world today. Where are you uncomfortable with it? Where do you need to explore?

Take 30 minutes for these drawings, then divide into triads, sit down facing each other and allow each participant five minutes in which to explain his/her maps to the other two. Indicate the changes you have made over the years, how you feel about those changes, and how well your present map is serving you.

In the total group take a few minutes to share feelings that this exercise evoked and to summarize any learnings that came out of it.

BREAK: (10 minutes)

Exercise 2: Resources for Map Revising (15 minutes)

In the total group brainstorm the encouragements and the re-sources you have experienced in the process of revising your maps of reality. Put each contribution on newsprint as a way of reinforc-ing the learning.

In one session we came up with these suggestions (see next page):

WHAT HELPS US UPDATE OUR MAPS?

Getting feedback from others (and really listening to it)

Becoming aware that our maps *need* updating

Asking "says who?" of inherited beliefs

Getting into therapy

Being aware of pain/bad feelings

Reading books from different points of view

Exploring our intuitions

Trying alternative routes

Releasing old resentments

Checking other people's maps

Checking our assumptions

Developing new relationships

Owning our strengths and powers

Being open to challenge

This is an appropriate time to refer to the Jo-Hari Window (p. 42) and discuss the processes of self-disclosure and feedback that can enlarge our understanding of ourselves and others.

Exercise 3: Inside and Out (30 minutes)

We have worked with our "maps" of outer reality. Now let's focus on our perceptions of our own inner world.

Give each participant a sheet of construction paper and crayons. For five minutes create on one side of the paper a face mask (cutting holes for eyes) with images and words to represent how you want to appear to other people. Turn the paper over and for five minutes write and draw on the inside of the mask how you actually appear to yourself. Be ruthlessly honest.

When everyone is ready, stand up and in silence mill around holding the outside of your masks in front of your face so that others can "read" them. After each person has had a chance to view everyone else's mask, choose partners, sit down facing each other and take turns sharing the feelings that were aroused during this exercise. Share as little or much as you wish of what you put on the inside of your mask representing how you actually see yourself. What feelings does this arouse? What determines how much you will withhold or reveal? Where are the discrepancies between how you want others to perceive you and how you perceive yourself? Would you like to be totally open about yourself with someone else?

Come back into the total group and share for ten minutes whatever learnings you may wish from both exercises in this session. (You may wish, instead, to close the exercise in this way: In silence, one partner closes his eyes while the other gently touches his face and says, "I see you; I hear you." Still in silence, partners repeat the process in reverse.)

CLOSURE: This exercise may be used again in the group's closing circle, changing the words to "I *want* to see you; I *want* to hear you." Let one person turn and face the person to his/her left, repeating these words; then as that person goes on around the circle, let the second person follow, and the third, and so on, until everyone has faced each other group member, thus making personal contact with everyone in the group.

ASSIGNMENT: Read pages 64–78 in *The Road Less Traveled* and do the exercises beginning on page 47.

SESSION FIVE: Balancing
Pages 64–78 in *The Road Less Traveled*

GOALS OF THIS SESSION: (1) To examine the tensions of life that call for "flexible responses," and (2) the stages of life that demand "giving up" what is no longer appropriate behavior if we are to grow.

MATERIALS NEEDED: Newsprint, marker, writing paper, pens or pencils.

SUMMARY OF CONTENT: Discipline itself must be disciplined, and this quality of discipline Scott Peck calls "balancing." Balancing is "the extraordinary capacity to flexibly strike and continually re-strike a delicate balance between conflicting needs, goals, duties, responsibilities, directions, etc."

Growth demands that we give up inappropriate patterns of behavior, personality traits, ideologies and life-styles, which can be extremely painful. Depression can be expected to accompany such giving up and is a sign that a process of growth has begun internally and is calling us to move on.

One form of giving up is what Peck calls "bracketing"—the act of temporarily putting one's self aside to observe one's behavior objectively and/or to incorporate strange and new aspects into one's self. But one must have a self—a sense of identity and worth— before it can be given up.

GETTING STARTED: (10 minutes) Allow your usual opening minutes for persons to share what has happened to them during the week, what learnings they have experienced, or what feelings they need to "get off their chests" in order to move on into new material.

Exercise 1: The Polarities of Life (15 minutes)

You may want to introduce this exercise by recalling the fact that Peck sets the need for flexibility against the background of two realities: (1) that life comes to us as a series of polarities (which one group preferred to speak of as tensions), and (2) that growth is a movement from one stage of development to another.

Spend a few minutes listing on newsprint some of the specific polarities of life that cause us to live in tension. Begin with Peck's first three disciplines, pointing out the polarities they represent. In one group, the newsprint read:

LIFE'S POLARITIES

Gratification
Delay . . . . Spontaneity

Responsibility
Over-responsible . . . . Under-responsible

Reality
Completely honest . . . . Withholding Truth
Punctuality . . . . Casualness
Adult . . . . Child
Masculine . . . . Feminine
Work . . . . Play
Self-denial . . . . Self-indulgence
Reflection . . . . Activity
Solitude . . . . Gregariousness

Spend a few minutes discussing the mindset required to live within the tension of such polarities. Compare it to walking a tightrope, or to getting the right tension on violin strings to play beautiful music. Put the group's ideas on another sheet of newsprint.

One newsprint contained these responses:

TO LIVE WITH OPTIMUM TENSION IS:

- to embrace opposites as equally necessary
- to live with both-ands more than either-ors
- to keep open minded and forego "premature closure"
- to decide each issue on its own merits, weighing pros and cons carefully
- to believe that balance is tenuous and transitory, knowing it must be constantly adjusted and readjusted
- to believe there is no static balance; it is always dynamic and changing

---

Exercise 2: *Where I Feel the Tug of War* (20 minutes)

Invite participants to self-select into triads and, giving each other equal time, share the particular polarities they are aware of in their own lives, what they are finding helpful in living within those tensions, where they feel the need for help, and what changes they would like to make in their behavior. You may wish to pull back together in a total group to briefly hear any discoveries that have been made in this process.

BREAK: (10 minutes)

Exercise 3: *The Stages of Life* (30 minutes)

Scott Peck, on page 71, refers to Erik Erikson's eight stages of life, each having its developmental tasks and its "growth crisis." The diagram on pages 56–57, amplifying nine stages of life, is adapted from that of the famous Harvard professor, which has been almost universally accepted as a description of the stages through which most individuals normally pass in their growth to maturity.

Be sure to emphasize (1) that failure to develop successfully from one stage to the next leaves "unfinished business" that can complicate dealing with the next tasks on life's agenda, and (2) that moving on to the next stage requires letting go of the security of the previous stage, just as a trapeze artist must let go of the security of one trapeze before he or she can reach for the next. There is risk in growth.

You may want to put the words of a familiar poster on newsprint at this point: "You can fly, but first the cocoon has to go!"

Ask each participant to take his or her journal and for ten minutes write about two subjects: (1) What are some of the major "letting go's" you have accomplished? How did you feel at the time? Did you allow yourself to mourn losses? Have you completed the mourning process? How have you grown from the experiences? and (2) Where and what are you needing to give up *now* in order to grow? What life stage are you in? What are the tasks facing you? What help do you need? What are you willing to do?

Exercise 4: My Next Move (30 minutes)

Let participants self-select into diads. As they sit facing each other, invite participants to take five minutes each sharing presently felt needs for "letting go" of the old and moving into newness in particular areas of life. When each person has spoken, divide the remainder of the time for responses to what each has heard, from the others.

Avoid giving each other advice. You may ask questions for clarification or repeat back what you heard in your own words and offer support and encouragement. If you are comfortable doing so, hold each other's hands and pray for each other silently or aloud, as you risk changes that will bring both loss and gain to each of your lives.

CLOSURE: As you form your closing circle, suggest that participants place their arms around each other's shoulders. Let this symbolize the solidarity of the group and the support you are giving each other as one by one you "walk the tightrope" of balancing competing interests and give up securities that are no longer appropriate to your stage of development.

ASSIGNMENT: Read pages 81–97 in *The Road Less Traveled* and do the exercises beginning on page 59.

SESSION SIX: *On Love*
Pages 81–97 in *The Road Less Traveled*

GOALS OF THIS SESSION: (1) To define true love, (2) to distinguish it from "falling in love" and "romantic love," and (3) to confront our own "loving" behavior.

MATERIALS NEEDED: Newsprint, marker, pens and paper, tape or record player and appropriate background music for reflection time.

SUMMARY OF CONTENT: Love is the motive and energy to discipline ourselves, which no one can define fully and adequately, but which, in Scott Peck's scheme of things, is defined as "the will to extend one's self for the purpose of nurturing one's own or another's spiritual growth."

Love of self and love of others are inseparable, one reinforcing the other. Both imply effort (extending oneself) and purpose (spiritual growth). They are acts of will and are clearly to be distinguished from "falling in love." Acts of real love are often performed without feelings of love. They are "enlarging experiences," whereas falling in love has little to do with spiritual development.

There is a process of attraction and incorporation called *cathexis*, which is not love but can open the door for love and can also embrace objects and activities. Real love occurs only between persons.

GETTING STARTED: (5 minutes) As people gather, take a few minutes to share any unfinished business from the previous session, or any feelings that need to be reported before you look at the goals for this session.

Exercise 1: Sharing Answers (15 minutes)

Run through the list of statements participants were to mark true or false in their workbooks (page 61) to see what responses they made. (All the statements are true and are based on Peck's statements in this section.)

After a brief discussion of Peck's concepts, move on to the next exercise in which actual experiences are to be shared. Together, these two exercises will prepare the way for Exercise 3 in which you will come to terms with Peck's precise definition of love.

Exercise 2: Ten Questions (30 minutes)

Divide your group in half and form two lines facing each other (or two circles, one inside the other) so that each person is facing a partner. Allow a minute and a half for each person to share his or her answer to the following questions. Every three minutes, then, participants will rotate and pair off with a different individual, allowing interaction with a large number of persons in the group. (For each turn have each person move two spaces to the left, moving around the end when it is reached and it will work smoothly.)

Call out the first question clearly. Call time after a minute and a half, and at the end of three minutes have people rotate. Call out the second question and repeat the process.

1. Describe your first "crush."
2. Describe an experience in which you felt loved by your mother.
3. Describe an experience of "falling out of love."
4. Describe your love for some object or activity.
5. Describe early messages you received about sexuality.
6. Describe an experience in which you felt loved by your father.
7. Tell about an adult who loved you as a child.
8. Describe your first date.
9. Describe an experience of unrequited love.
10. What myths of romantic love did you grow up with?

Come back together as a total group and share the messages that were given you about love as you were growing up. What was modeled by your parents and teachers? What did your own experiences suggest to you? Then put on newsprint your "myths" about "falling in love" and "romantic love" as contrasted with true love in the sense that Peck describes it.

One list included such comments as this:

LOVE LASTS, IF IT'S THE REAL THING!

IF YOU'RE IN LOVE YOU WON'T BE ATTRACTED TO ANYONE ELSE.

THERE IS JUST ONE PERSON IN ALL THE WORLD FOR ME, AND GOD WILL SHOW ME WHO IT IS IF I PRAY AND WAIT.

LOVE AND MARRIAGE WILL COMPLETE ME AND VALIDATE ME AS A PERSON.

LOVE MAKES EVERYTHING BEAUTIFUL.

THE RIGHT PARTNER WILL MEET ALL MY NEEDS.

IF NOT, I CAN CHANGE HIM/HER AFTER WE MARRY.

IF HE/SHE REALLY LOVES ME, HE'LL KNOW WHAT I WANT WITHOUT MY HAVING TO ASK FOR IT.

BREAK: (10 minutes)

Exercise 3: Defining Love (20 minutes)

Coming back from the break, spend a short time reviewing Peck's definition of love. Share how you *feel* about it and whether you agree. Recall what Peck says about "ego boundaries": their development, how "falling in love" collapses them and how true love expands them, even to the possibility of embracing the universe in mystical unity. Refer back to Exercise 3 in the participants' workbooks for what they have written about this.

Exercise 4: How Am I Loving? (35 minutes)

Invite each participant, alone and in silence (while you play some soft music, without words, as a background, perhaps) to reflect on three questions. Do not announce or display the questions all at once. Give time for reflection on the first question before displaying the second, and time on the second before displaying the third.

155

1. How am I extending myself to nurture my own spiritual growth?
2. How am I extending myself to nurture someone else's spiritual growth?
3. Where am I dissatisfied with my present state of loving?

After a few minutes encourage participants to choose one relationship and write a letter to that person (it may be oneself or even God), saying whatever you wish about the relationship and how you would like to see it changed. You may wish to write a dialogue. If so, let flow whatever you want to say to the person. Then write the answer that flows through your pen, without attempting to control it. Write your response and let the dialogue flow back and forth as it will.

Spend the last few minutes in groups of three, giving each person time to share whatever decisions may have emerged during this exercise, if it is comfortable to do so.

CLOSING CIRCLE: Form a circle, holding hands or with arms around each other's shoulders. Give participants an opportunity to share briefly what the evening's experience has meant to them. Thank them for their participation, and have someone read aloud the apostle Paul's magnificent description of love and spiritual growth in I Corinthians 13:4–13.

ASSIGNMENT: Read pages 98–131 in *The Road Less Traveled* and do the exercises beginning on page 67.

SESSION SEVEN: *What Love Isn't and Is*
Pages 98–131 in *The Road Less Traveled*

GOALS OF THIS SESSION: (1) To distinguish dependency, "cathecting" and feelings of love from "willing" love, and (2) to practice giving attention.

MATERIALS NEEDED: Newsprint, marker, paper, pens or pencils.

SUMMARY OF CONTENT: Love is not dependency. In fact, "two people love each other only when they are quite capable of living without each other, but *choose* to live with each other." Dependency forms fierce attachments, but it destroys rather than builds relationships. True love leads to growth—growth of the lover as well as the loved. It is a self-replenishing activity, and in a sense a selfish one.

Love is not cathecting, which is an attachment to objects. We can love only human beings but even human beings can be treated as objects rather than persons.

Love is not self-sacrifice. To nurture the growth of others does not diminish ourselves. Rather, it results in our own nurture and growth.

Love is not a feeling; it is an act of willing, though it is a happy conjunction when accompanied by "feelings of love."

Love is always either work or courage—work when it overcomes laziness; courage when it counteracts fear. It is giving attention, and the most important way in which we can exercise our attention is by listening, which demands total concentration.

GETTING STARTED: (10 minutes) You have come to the midpoint in a 12-session course. After allowing participants a chance to "check in," it could be a healthy exercise to ask participants for an evaluation of their experience so far. What has been most helpful to them? What would they like more of in the remaining sessions? This can be done by handing out paper and pencils, asking them to write briefly and anonymously, then folding and gathering the papers for examination by the leaders afterward.

Every group of persons has its own uniqueness. It is important to take periodic readings and to be governed, in part at least, by their wishes as you plan each session.

Spend a few minutes discussing the statements in Exercise 1 of the participants' workbook (pages 68–69). These are statements taken directly from *The Road Less Traveled* and a key to the answers and page numbers of the quotations follows this section.

Exercise 1: Dependency and Me (30 minutes)

Spend a few minutes discussing the distinctions Peck makes between true love and dependency, cathecting, self-sacrifice and "feelings of love." You may wish to quote the statement attributed to Reinhold Niebuhr: "We are meant to love people and use things, not love things and use people."

Peck defines love as an extension of the will. Can feelings be willed? Can we *decide* to like someone? Feelings simply "are." But we can will to act in certain ways apart from our feelings. We can love someone whom we don't like. And we can acknowledge our duty to love God, to love our neighbor, to love each other, to love our enemy, indeed, to love ourselves—in other words, to act in ways that nourish spiritual growth whether or not we feel "loving" at the moment.

Explain to your group that your concentration during this first hour is going to be on seeing the distinction between love and dependency. Then move on to the following exercise.

Let participants self-select partners, sit down facing each other, decide who will be person A and let that person begin saying to person B, "What I like about being dependent is . . ." completing the statement, then repeating it and completing it in a different way, and continuing thus for a minute and a half.

For example, person A may say, "What I like about being dependent is knowing that supper will be ready for me when I get home. What I like about being dependent is that Sally handles all the finances. What I like. . . ."

Person B is not to respond, but simply listen, without interrupting. The leader will call time after a minute and a half, and then person B will have his or her turn.

When this process is completed person A will repeat, for a minute and a half, "What I *don't* like about being dependent is . . ." and keep completing that sentence until his time is up, whereupon person B will have equal time.

In the remaining time encourage partners to share the feelings they experienced during this exercise and any awareness that was reinforced by it or that came as a discovery. In the total group report in anything of interest.

In one group a participant said, "It was hard to get started, but once I really felt heard by my partner, I wanted to go on and on."

A variation of this exercise that you might want to experiment with is to repeat the process using the statements, "What I like about having others dependent on me is . . ." and "What I don't like about having others dependent on me is. . . ."

Exercise 2: How Am I Doing? (20 minutes)

In the total group, share some of the learnings that came from Exercise 1. You may wish to distinguish different modes of dependency, such as physical, emotional, financial, vocational, and so on, and recognize the validity of each of these at particular times and in particular situations, as well as the inappropriateness of the same dependencies at different times and in different situations. You might wish to refer back to the diagram on pages 56–57 of the participants' workbook describing the process of growing from the total dependency of infancy to the autonomy of adulthood.

It is well to recognize too that there are times when one regresses to a place of dependency temporarily, such as with physical illness, emotional trauma that accompany the loss of a job, of a friendship, of a loved one, and so on.

Total independence is an illusion. We can no more live without getting our emotional, financial and vocational needs met than we can live without air, food and rest. The ideal is *interdependence* that strikes a healthy balance between legitimate dependency needs and the need for autonomy.

What are some legitimate dependency needs and what are some legitimate ways of going about getting them met? Let participants return to the diads of Exercise 1 and share both how the growing-up process has been for them, how they get their legitimate needs met, and what changes they would like to make in significant personal relationships. (Display these instructions on newsprint.)

BREAK: (10 minutes)

Exercise 3: Accurate Listening (45 minutes)

Go over with your group the principles for true listening that are found on page 70 of the workbook, so that participants will have in mind some of the basic guidelines on what to do and what not to do as they begin intentionally practicing the principles. Use a role play to demonstrate good listening skills. Let several group members take turns practicing before the group and getting feedback.

Let participants divide into diads, sit facing each other and decide who will go first. For three minutes invite person A to talk about how the issues of dependency and independence impinge on a present significant relationship. Be specific and factual. Do not theorize; simply describe the situation as it is. Meanwhile, person B is to listen intently, without interrupting, evaluating or judging. Be aware of feeling tone, body language, etc.

After three minutes, person B is to repeat back to person A in other words what he or she has heard, until person A is satisfied that he has truly been understood.

Following this, person B is to have three minutes to describe a present significant relationship followed by person A's response until person B is satisfied he has really been heard.

Following this, ask participants to be quiet, to shut their eyes, and to reflect on what this experience has meant to them. Then ask them to share with each other their feelings and learnings about listening and being heard.

For the remaining minutes encourage them to write about a significant relationship and the quality of listening/hearing that exists within it. What changes would they like to see? What might they do to enable change?

Come back together as a total group to share feelings and learnings briefly.

CLOSURE: Does the circle, arms around each other's shoulders, seem comfortable now to you and your group? It is a good place to express appreciation, to close with prayer, or to wish each other well during the coming week.

ASSIGNMENT: Read pages 131–55 in *The Road Less Traveled* and do the exercises beginning on page 75 in preparation for the next session.

Key to answers and page numbers for Exercise 1 in the workbook:

a. TRUE Page 83	i. FALSE Page 117
b. TRUE Page 98	j. TRUE Page 111
c. FALSE Page 98	k. TRUE Page 89
d. TRUE Page 104	l. TRUE Page 111
e. FALSE Page 105	m. TRUE Page 88, 118
f. FALSE Page 98	n. TRUE Page 111, 119
g. FALSE Page 119	o. TRUE Page 116
h. FALSE Page 110	

SESSION EIGHT: *The Courage of Love*
Pages 131–55 in *The Road Less Traveled*

GOAL OF THIS SESSION: To identify and face the risks of loving, particularly the risks of confrontation and commitment.

MATERIALS NEEDED: Newsprint, marker, paper and pens or pencils.

SUMMARY OF CONTENT: As we turn from the *work* of love to the *courage* of love, Scott Peck reminds us that in extending ourselves in love we face certain risks. He names four of them.

To love is to risk *loss*. Those whom we love may let us down or leave us, but not to love is not to "live" at all.

Another risk is that of *growing up*—of daring to be different, asserting our independence, and being true to what is within us. Only by asserting our freedom can we enlarge our lives.

A third risk is that of *commitment*—what enables us to move beyond "falling in love" to genuine love and gives constancy to a relationship. But permanence can never be guaranteed.

The final risk is that of *confrontation*. If we truly love another, we will at times offer criticism and wisdom that we believe will nurture spiritual growth.

GETTING STARTED: (10 minutes) Come prepared to report to participants the results of the mid-course evaluation papers they wrote at the last session, if you chose to do it that way. Be sure to express appreciation for their responses, and make any "course corrections" that seem appropriate and mutually acceptable.

If there is time, let participants report briefly their learnings over the past week. Go over the goals for this session.

Exercise 1: Creative Confrontation (15 minutes)

Begin this session with a quick summary of the four risks that Scott Peck presents, and explain that this session's agenda will concentrate on the last two.

In a brainstorming session with the entire group, ask participants to suggest guidelines for healthy confrontation. Put their suggestions on newsprint but do not analyze or discuss them until all suggestions have been recorded.

One group suggested the following:

HELPFUL CONFRONTATION

There must be a relationship to begin with.
Do it privately, one to one.
The climate must be a climate of caring.
Suggest one's behavior needs changing, not the person.
Express feelings, not judgments; how you feel, not how they fail.
Own the intensity of your feelings.

Exercise 2: Caring to Confront (40 minutes)

Divide into triads for an exercise in which each person will rehearse an actual confrontation with someone you care about in real life with whom you are in real conflict. Identify yourselves as persons A, B, and C. Person A will confront person B first while person C observes from the side. Take a few minutes to let person A identify the person, the specific situation, your feelings about it and what change you wish.

While person A describes the situation prompting the confron-

163

tation, person B will "get into" the thoughts and feelings of person A's antagonist, so that in the actual confrontation, person B can role-play that person as closely as possible.

When you are ready to begin, person A will confront his real life antagonist whose role is being played by person B, and B will respond in character while person C sits silently observing. Call time after 5 minutes. Let person C share observations, then discuss as a triad the effectiveness of the confrontation and how it might be improved. Allow 5 minutes for this.

In round two, person B will confront person C while A observes.

In round three, person C will confront person A while B observes.

Take a few minutes in triads to share what the experience meant to each person, then come back together as a total group and add to the brainstorming list any new suggestions for improving one's skill in confronting learned during the exercise. One group added these suggestions:

> Rehearse beforehand with a third party.
> Invite a third party to observe or arbitrate.
> Examine yourself more than the other person.
> Use "I feel" statements rather than "you do" statements.
> Say, "I care about you *and*," not "I care about you *but*."
> Say, "I care about you, about me, and about our relationship."
> Put yourself in the other person's place.

BREAK: (10 minutes)

Exercise 3: Memories of Constancy (10 minutes)

Have each person sit comfortably and relaxed with eyes closed, breathing deeply and evenly. In complete silence, repeat these words slowly, deliberately: "Go back in your memory to early childhood. Recall the house or apartment you lived in . . . your place in that house . . . the members of your family. . . . (Use all your senses: sight . . . hearing . . . smell . . . touch) your feelings about the others . . . and about yourself." (Pause for 10 seconds between each statement.)

"Recall any memories you have of constancy, or the lack of it . . . being able to depend on others . . . their being there for you when you needed them. . . . How did you experience dependability? Where did you want it but not experience it? . . . Stay with each memory long enough to recall the feelings you experienced at the time." (Pause for a minute.)

"Move on through your childhood . . . (30-second pause) to your teenage years . . . (30-second pause) to young adulthood . . . (pause) and on up to the present time . . . (pause)." Do not rush this experience, but when you feel people have had sufficient time, invite them to open their eyes and return to the room where you are meeting. Some deep feelings may be evoked by this exercise. Some people may cry or groan. Don't be upset by any display of emotions, and don't try to smooth them over in an artificial way. Let people have their feelings. Wait quietly for them to subside.

Exercise 4: Journaling on Commitment (25 minutes)

Invite participants to take paper and pen or pencil and write about the subject of commitment using the following questions as guidelines. (Put them on newsprint for all to see.)

1. What examples and messages was I given on commitment as I grew up?
2. Who is committed to me and in what ways?
3. To whom or what am I committed?
4. Where/how am I wanting to be (more) committed?
5. What is standing in my way?

Write for 15 minutes, then choose a partner whom you have come to trust, sit facing each other and, taking turns, share what you wish to of your feelings, hopes, difficulties, and intentions regarding committed relationships.

In the total group, report in whatever discoveries have come to you through this experience. It is not necessary to describe specific situations. The purpose of this "wrap up" is to crystallize the learnings from which all can profit.

CLOSURE: In your closing circle you may wish to read aloud the anonymous words found on page 80 of the participants' workbook.

ASSIGNMENT: Read pages 155–82 in *The Road Less Traveled* and do the exercises beginning on page 85.

SESSION NINE: *The Discipline of Love*
Pages 155–82 in *The Road Less Traveled*

GOALS OF THIS SESSION: (1) To explore how to both recognize and manage our feelings and (2) how to love others by respecting their separateness.

MATERIALS NEEDED: Newsprint, marker, paper, pencils or pens.

SUMMARY OF CONTENT: Loving relationships, Peck says, are disciplined relationships, but not to the suppression of deep and passionate feelings. Feelings energize us for the work of living, but we need to manage them carefully lest they control and enslave us.

"Genuine love not only respects the individuality of the other, but actually seeks to cultivate it, even at the risk of separation or loss." And love is the key to healing relationships as well as spiritual growth, whether practiced by a professional psychotherapist or any loving individual. Any truly loving relationship will be therapeutic.

GETTING STARTED: (10 minutes) Go around the circle asking group members to name what they are honestly feeling (noting that "good" and "bad" are not feelings but judgments). When everyone has spoken, ask how difficult that was, by way of leading into the opening exercise.

Exercise 1: Feeling My Feelings (10 minutes)

Identify as many feelings as possible in an initial time of brainstorming. Let group members call out feelings as you put them on newsprint. Ask how we can know what we are feeling (recognizing that some may be out of touch with particular feelings or feelings in general).

Put some basic principles about feelings on newsprint for discussion. Here is a suggested list to which you may want to make additions:

1. Feelings aren't good or bad; they simply are. (It's what we do with them that can be destructive or constructive.)
2. We feel them in our bodies. (Observe how totally children express feelings through their bodies.)
3. We learn to hide unacceptable feelings and in their place show feelings that we are *taught* are acceptable, thus getting out of touch with our own true feelings. (Sometimes our bodies get tight and our breathing is shallow as a result.)
4. Only when we are aware of our feelings can we make them work for us. (So we need practice in reconnecting with our feelings in a safe environment.)

Experiment with having the group act out some basic feelings. (In the language of Transactional Analysis, there are four basic feelings: *Mad*, *Sad*, *Glad*, and *Afraid*.) Have group members stand, shut their eyes, breathe easily, loose any constricting wearing apparel, and act out, by taking appropriate postures, using appropriate gestures and uttering appropriate sounds and words, the four basic emotions. Begin with sadness for one minute, then fear, then anger, and finally gladness. In the total group report in reactions to the exercise before moving on to the next.

Exercise 2: Managing My Emotions (30 minutes)

Begin by reading Peck's statement on page 156: "I frequently tell my patients that their feelings are their slaves and that the art of self-discipline is like the art of slave-owning." What reactions does that stimulate? Take time to hear responses, then ask, "In general, do you need greater control of your feelings or greater spontaneity?" After a moment ask what emotion seems most difficult to deal with. Most individuals are likely to suggest *anger*. So ask your participants to reflect on how they deal with their anger.

Place a sign on one wall reading "Over-controlled," and on the opposite wall one reading, "Completely spontaneous." Pretend there is a line running from one wall to the other and ask participants to stand and place themselves where they belong on the continuum.

Take a few minutes to let participants share why they made the choice they did. Encourage discussion and sharing of ways that some have found to express their feelings appropriately.

Ask, for example, whether it is possible to be both angry and loving toward the same person? At the same time? Can one express anger but temper it with expressions of caring, thus making it safe to deal constructively with the anger?

Repeat this exercise with the other three basic emotions.

For the remaining time, self-select into twosomes and encourage each person to share the emotion he or she has most difficulty with. Where do you want more spontaneity? More control? What specific steps might you take to change your usual behavior?

If you wish, bring the group back together and put on newsprint any significant learnings that came out of this exercise.

BREAK: (10 minutes)

Exercise 2: Who Has Loved Me? (10 minutes)

Take a few minutes to think who the people are (in your recent or remote past) who have truly loved you. Recall specific *ways* they showed their love. Let people call them out and put them on newsprint for all to see.

One paper read like this:

HOW I'VE BEEN LOVED

An adult gave a party just for me when I was a child.
My daughter paid my way to a workshop.
A friend held me when I needed to cry.
My mother groomed me with a lot of touching and evident pride.
I have a friend who confronts me creatively.
She loves me when I am my most unlovable.

Exercise 3: Love and Separateness (30 minutes)

Divide into diads making sure you are with someone you were not paired with in Exercise 1. Sit facing each other. Decide who will

169

be person A and who person B. For two minutes person A is to ask person B, "Who are you?" When person B replies, A is to repeat the question and keep repeating it after each answer from B, to elicit more and more information about person B's uniqueness.

It might be well for two leaders to model such an interaction. For example,

"Who are you?" . . . "I'm a sensitive, caring person."

"Who are you?" . . . "I like to go boating."

"Who are you?" . . . "I'm a lover of symphony music."

When the time is up the process is reversed, with B asking A for two minutes, "Who are you?" After that, have both participants close their eyes and in silence reflect on all they heard the other person say. After a moment or two, person A is to say to person B a series of statements beginning with, "If I really loved you, I would . . .," completing the sentence, then repeating it again and again, completing it each time with another expression of what he or she would do, "if I really loved you." Do this for three minutes. Then reverse the process, with B repeating the statement to A.

When both persons have been heard and responded to, let them take a few minutes to share the feelings the exercise evoked and to express appreciation to each other.

Take the few remaining minutes to come back together as a total group and share any significant learnings that came out of the experience.

Exercise 4: A Significant Relationship (15 minutes)

Take some time for individual journaling. Alone and in silence (unless you wish to play some instrumental music quietly in the background), let each person reflect on a significant present relationship and the issue of separateness as it relates to it. Describe the relationship. How is separateness recognized and honored? What are your feelings about it? Your learnings? Your wants?

CLOSURE: In your closing circle you may wish to have someone read aloud Kahlil Gibran's words on separateness which are quoted by Peck on page 169 of *The Road Less Traveled*. Or, you may wish to once again go around the circle and ask people to express their *feelings* about the session.

ASSIGNMENT: Read pages 185–232 in *The Road Less Traveled* and do the exercises beginning on page 95.

SESSION TEN: Growth and Religion
Pages 185–232 in *The Road Less Traveled*

GOALS OF THIS SESSION: (1) To explore the meaning of spiritual growth and (2) to identify the beliefs by which we live.

MATERIALS NEEDED: Newsprint, 8½-by-11-inch heavy white paper and markers for everyone, pens or pencils.

SUMMARY OF CONTENT: Everyone has a religion, or a world view, though we often are largely unaware of how we view the world. Our beliefs are conditioned by our culture and our families of origin. Spiritual growth is an expansion of our earliest beliefs that we need constantly to revise and extend.

One's earliest memory often "captures the essence of one's world view." One's growth is often from unquestioning acceptance to questioning nonacceptance, to experiences of mystery and growth into certainty and a more personal relationship to God.

Second-hand information won't do. Each of us must develop a

171

"wholly personal religion," though this involves questioning, forsaking and honest searching. "If there were one thing I could hope for the reader," Peck concludes, "it would be the capacity to perceive the miraculous."

GETTING STARTED: (10 minutes) You may wish to begin by asking who feels free to report their earliest memory (which they recorded in Exercise 1 of the participants' workbook) and any significance they may have discovered in it.

Exercise 1: What Is Spiritual Growth? (40 minutes)

Throughout the course so far we have been following Scott Peck's description of a process that has as its outcome "spiritual growth." Up to this point, however, spiritual growth has not been defined. It is time at last to become aware of how Peck defines it. But first let's focus on our own understanding and experience of spiritual growth.

Ask each participant to write "what spiritual growth means to me," while you display on newsprint the following categories that may be helpful to them: "Its goal . . . Its process . . . Resources I find helpful." Give them ten minutes to work alone and in silence.

Now give each participant a sheet of heavy paper and a marker and ask them to write a brief *definition* of spiritual growth to be shared presently with the whole group. Have them write in large enough print to be read from three feet away. When they have completed this, have them stand up and mill around, holding their definitions in front of them. Mill until everyone has had a chance to read what others have written.

At this point you may wish to point out how Peck defines spiritual growth (though much of the description of it does not appear until the section on Grace).

On page 283 Peck says, "Spiritual growth is the attainment of godhood by the conscious self." By this he seems to mean "oneness with God" in the sense of claiming our rightful power and using it responsibly. Spend a few minutes in discussion. Then move on to sharing the *process* of growth as group members experience it, listing their input on newsprint.

In all likelihood two movements will be discerned: *taking hold* and *letting go*. Ask participants to decide which their growth has emphasized more—letting go in surrender or taking hold of one's life to grow spiritually. Make them choose, and form two groups, one on each side of the room. Have each group form a circle and tell each other why they chose as they did.

Some may find it difficult or impossible to choose between these two positions, so let them form a third group and caucus.

After a few minutes, have the first two groups face each other, while the third group stands to one side. Invite groups one and two to talk to each other, one person at a time, sharing their personal experience in explaining why they chose as they did. After a number have spoken invite the third group to enter the conversation.

In the total group take a few minutes to share resources that different individuals have found helpful to their spiritual growth.

BREAK: (10 minutes)

Exercise 2: The Growth of One's Beliefs (10 minutes)

One significant aspect of the process we have been describing is the formulation of one's beliefs in a "world view" or a "religion" that can be expressed in statements of belief. As Peck says, everyone inherits such a belief system from one's family and one's culture. But it is essential that everyone develop his or her own "wholly personal religion." And that, typically, follows a four-step process.

Display the following scheme on newsprint for all to see:

> 1. Unquestioning acceptance, to
> 2. Questioning nonacceptance, to
> 3. The experience of mystery, to
> 4. Some certainty of beliefs.

Invite brief discussion about this scheme and what Peck has to say about science and religion. Invite each participant to reflect for a few moments on where he or she is right now in the process.

Exercise 3: A Crisis of Beliefs (30 minutes)

Display on newsprint the following from the words by Clarence Jordan quoted in the participants' workbook: "Our English word be-lief comes from the old Anglo Saxon *be* which means 'by' and *lief* which means 'life.' What one lives by is actually his belief or his *by-life*."

Give participants paper and pen or pencil and ask them to write for three or four minutes a number of their beliefs as they come to their minds. Do not elaborate on them, or evaluate them. Simply write them down, one after the other, putting on paper all that they can of what has value to them. Don't write what you think you *ought* to believe, or what you *wish* you could believe, but what you actually *do* believe. What are your operational beliefs—the beliefs by which you actually live?

Call time and let the leader declare that there is a faith crisis, just like the energy crisis of a few years ago when gasoline was in short supply. Because of the crisis, participants will be allowed only three beliefs. They are to go through their lists and select the three that are most important to them. It is permissible to change or edit anything that has been written previously or to add something new that comes to mind.

Write these three beliefs on 8½-by-11-inch sheets of white paper in large enough letters to be read three feet away, and when all are ready, ask each person to hold his beliefs in front of him while the group mills around the room reading what each other has written. When that has been accomplished, let each person choose someone with whom he or she would like to dialogue. Claim a space, sit down facing each other and share the meaning of your beliefs, the importance of them to you, and how they actually affect your behavior from day to day. Is there a gap between your beliefs and behavior that you would like to modify?

What discoveries came to you through this exercise? Share them with your partner. Spend whatever time remains in the larger group sharing feelings and learnings from this experience.

Exercise 4: *Where I Want to Grow* (10 minutes)

Encourage participants to spend some time journaling, in silence, on the following questions:
1. Where am I in my process of spiritual growth and beliefs?
2. In what ways do I wish to change?
3. What is helping me or hindering me from growing?

CLOSURE: In your closing circle, encourage participants to share briefly, from their journaling time, one way in which they wish to grow and what they plan to do about it in the coming week. Offer these intentions as a prayer, either spoken or in silence.

ASSIGNMENT: Read pages 235–71 in *The Road Less Traveled* and do the exercises beginning on page 105 in preparation for the next session.

SESSION ELEVEN: The Miracles of Grace
Pages 235–71 in *The Road Less Traveled*

GOAL OF THIS SESSION: To explore the resources of Grace that are available to all of us.

MATERIALS NEEDED: Newsprint, marker, paper, pencils or pens.

SUMMARY OF CONTENT: In the final section of his book, Scott Peck argues for the existence of "a powerful force originating outside of human consciousness which nurtures the spiritual growth of human beings." This he calls Grace, and he offers four specific examples of what he describes as "miracles."

Health

In his practice of psychotherapy Peck has repeatedly observed a force in most of his patients that protects and fosters mental health, even under the most adverse conditions, which he attributes to God.

The Unconscious

A vast part of our minds is below our awareness but rich beyond imagination. It is accessible to us through dreams, idle thoughts and slips of the tongue. The unconscious needs to be explored for it is wiser than we are and is our interface with God.

Serendipity

Highly implausible events which come to us at crucial times and for our benefit are to be seen as miracles of Grace.

Evolution

Finally, "the growth process of all life itself" is a miracle, counteracting as it does the winding down force of entropy in all of nature. Spiritual growth, which is effortful and difficult, is the evolution of the individual.

From these miracles of Grace, Peck hypothesizes the existence of a God who loves us and wants us to grow.

GETTING STARTED: (10 minutes) Devote the usual opening few minutes to "settling in," reporting what has happened during the week, particularly as it bears on the goals for spiritual growth that participants claimed during the last session.

Exercise 1: The Miracle of Health (20 minutes)

On page 237 Peck says of his own practice, "One seldom sees patients who are not basically healthier mentally than their parents." Invite participants to test this assertion by self-selecting into triads and for ten minutes sharing their experiences and feelings about where they are growthwise in comparison to their parents. Come back together for five minutes to draw together whatever emerges from the interaction.

In one group there was reluctance to judge parents or compare ourselves with them. "How do we know," one man asked, "what they would have done, given our time and circumstances?" But there was strong agreement that conditions have evolved to the point where there are more options for most of us than our parents enjoyed. This, however, also brings greater difficulties. And how can we know, with our limited perspective, whether or not the world is getting better?

Alternative Exercise: The Miracle of the Unconscious (30 minutes)

You may find it more profitable to spend these 30 minutes sharing experiences of healing that support Peck's contention that a miraculous force is at work in spite of accidents and illnesses that come our way. Or you may wish to divide the time to allow for a brief consideration of both these issues.

Put on newsprint for all to see (or duplicate and hand out) a diagram similar to the one shown on the following page to differentiate the unconscious mind from the conscious. The "collective unconscious" is a term derived from psychologist C. G. Jung to describe the reservoir of wisdom we inherit from and share with the rest of the human race. Peck sees it as our interface with God, the source of self-knowledge and true wisdom.

The Conscious and Unconscious Mind

Sigmund Freud saw the personal unconscious as the repository of "the primitive, the antisocial and the evil within us." Thus repressed below the surface of consciousness, it resides uncomfortably, affecting our behavior in destructive ways until brought to the surface and somehow resolved.

Carl Jung went beyond Freud to suggest that there is a collective unconscious that contains not only repressed material but a wealth

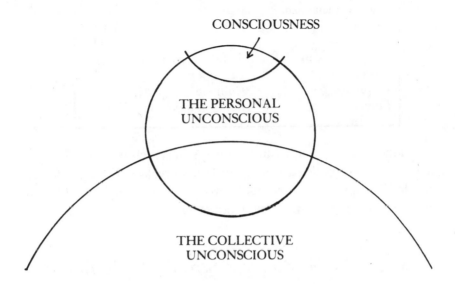

CONSCIOUSNESS

THE PERSONAL
UNCONSCIOUS

THE COLLECTIVE
UNCONSCIOUS

Consciousness represents only a tiny percentage of the contents of the human mind. Perhaps 95% of its content lies hidden in the unconscious until it protrudes in some way into consciousness or is deliberately encouraged to surface.

of inherited wisdom and insight that we share with all mankind and through which we come in contact with God. The unconscious, which at one point Peck identifies as God, is always ahead of the conscious mind, urging or beckoning it to grow. Mental health results from bringing the conscious mind into harmony with the unconscious.

Invite members of your group to suggest ways that the unconscious breaks into the conscious (beyond the ones Peck mentions on pp. 243–51). List ways we can open ourselves to the possibility. In one group we put the following on newsprint:

OPENING UP TO THE UNCONSCIOUS

Dreams	Music
Psychic phenomena	Fantasizing
Solitude	Moments of clarity (at par-
Meditation	ticular times of the day, like
Free association	first thing in the morning)
Journaling	Reflection
Hypnosis	Running
Prayer	Being in touch with nature

Allow time for "witnessing" to ways in which individual participants have experienced the unconscious breaking through, for example in significant dreams, through journaling, meditation,
answers to prayer or mystical experience.*

Exercise 3: The Miracle of Serendipity (10 minutes)

Allow time to share experiences of unexplainable coincidences that
support Peck's theory of Grace working on our behalf.

BREAK: (10 minutes)

Exercise 4: The Miracle of Evolution (30 minutes)

This exercise has three distinct parts. After putting on newsprint
a representation of the diagram on the forces of entropy and of

* Recommended books on dream interpretation and journaling include the following: On
dreams: Morton Kelsey, *Dreams, A Way To Listen to God* (New York: Paulist Press, 1978);
John A. Sanford, *Dreams and Healing* (New York: Paulist Press, 1978). On journaling:
Morton T. Kelsey, *Adventure Inward* (Minneapolis: Augsburg Publishing House, 1980); Ira
Progoff, *At a Journal Workshop* (New York: Dialogue House, 80 E. 11 St., 10003, 1975);
George F. Simons, *Keeping Your Personal Journal* (New York: Paulist Press, 1978).

growth (see *The Road Less Traveled*, p. 266), invite participants to journal for ten minutes on how, where and when they experience those forces in their own lives. Do this in silence while each person claims sufficient space to be undisturbed by others in the room.

After ten minutes come back together as a total group, make two lists on newsprint headed "Forces of Entropy" and "Forces of Grace" as participants call out specifics from their own experience.

One list looked like this:

FORCES OF ENTROPY	FORCES OF GRACE
"The world, the flesh and the devil"	Friends
Status expectations	Creating order
Overeating/self-indulgence	Forgiveness
Security/complacency	Spouse
Comparing/coveting	My heritage/family imprinting
Distrust/fear	Prayer
Discouragement	Music/art/beauty
Exhaustion	Laughter/play
Illness	The world/nature
Laziness	Books
Anger	Children
Poverty	Community
Cigarette smoking	Touch/massage
Lust	Affirmation and acceptance
Greed	
Resentment	

Let participants choose a partner whom they have come to know and trust and take equal time sharing the issues of the downward pull of entropy and the upward drive of Grace as they became aware of them in the journaling time. Be careful not to judge or evaluate each other. Rather, listen attentively, asking questions for clarification where necessary, suggesting options and alternatives and being supportive of each other in the struggle to grow spiritually.

Before concluding this session you may wish to raise the question of whether there are other miracles anyone wants to add to the four Peck identifies. "New birth," for example, is a term many use to describe a conversion experience that leads to a radical transformation of life. For some such a change may come gradually, almost imperceptibly. For others it may be sudden and dramatic.

Count Leo Tolstoy, for example, described his conversion thus: "I came to believe in Christ's teaching, and my life suddenly changed; I ceased to desire what I had previously desired, and began to desire what I formerly did not want. What had previously seemed to me good seemed evil, and what had seemed evil seemed good. It happened to me as it happens to a man who goes out on some business and on the way suddenly decides that the business is unnecessary and returns home. All that was on his right is now on his left, and all that was on his left is now on his right; his former wish to get as far as possible from home has changed into a wish to be as near as possible to it. The direction of my life and my desires became different, and good and evil changed places."

Some in your group may wish to share experiences of forgiveness and transformation briefly.

CLOSURE: In your closing circle you may wish to have someone read aloud the words of St. Augustine, quoted on pages 121–22 of the workbook.

ASSIGNMENT: Read pages 271–312 in *The Road Less Traveled* and do the exercises beginning on page 115.

SESSION TWELVE: *Resisting and Welcoming Grace*
Pages 271–312 in *The Road Less Traveled*

GOALS OF THIS SESSION: (1) To explore our resistances to Grace and the depth of our desire to grow spiritually, and (2) To summarize learnings from these twelve weeks and provide opportunity to say goodbye.

MATERIALS NEEDED: Newsprint, markers, paper, pens or pencils, crayons, masking tape.

SUMMARY OF CONTENT: The purpose of spiritual growth is an evolution of consciousness, a process of becoming one with God. But impediments lurk along the way, the chief of which is our laziness. Laziness, the opposite of love, is the "original sin" that dogs our tracks.

When we extend ourselves in love we are supported by Grace and move toward the goal in which God's life can produce in us "a new life form of God." This gives us the power to "know with God," "to make decisions with maximum awareness." But this power brings with it great responsibility, and so we fear it. Most people do not wish to make the supreme effort to grow to that place.

Grace is both earned and unearned. "We cannot will ourselves to grace, but we can by will open ourselves to its miraculous coming." How far we will go in spiritual growth is up to us.

GETTING STARTED: (20 minutes) If your group chooses to eat a potluck supper together, that in itself will provide the entrance into your final session. Recognize that endings bring loss and loss brings us to a place where we need to grieve. (A normal pattern of response is denial, then anger, bargaining and frustration and, finally, acceptance.) Allow for expressions of feeling about the ending of the course. Hopefully, some expressions of joy over new learning and growth and the making of new friends will balance the feelings of grief. Emphasize the goals of this final session.

Exercise 1: How Do I Resist Grace? (15 minutes)

Allow a few minutes in which to identify and acknowledge ways in which we resist Grace. Then have participants write a few of theirs on 8½-by-11-inch sheets of paper in words large enough to be read three feet away.

In one group we felt immediate resistance to this exercise and suggested that some might wish to head their list with, "I resist dealing with my resistances."

Holding these sheets in front of them, let everyone mill around the room reading what others have written.

When all have had the opportunity to read what each has written, you may wish to symbolically give up these resistances and put them behind you by burning them. Crumple up your sheets of paper and in some safe place (a fireplace, a large kettle, or the oven of your kitchen range) burn them as an expression of having "confessed" them and wishing to move beyond them.

BREAK: (10 minutes)

Exercise 2: What is Grace? (15 minutes)

Read aloud, or put on newsprint, the statement on page 308 of *The Road Less Traveled:* "While we cannot will ourselves to grace, we can by will open ourselves to its miraculous coming. We can prepare ourselves to be fertile ground, a welcoming place."

Invite participants to share what it means to them to experience Grace.

In one group people said things like this:

"Grace just *is*. I can't create it, but I need to be aware of it."

"It's like the air we breathe. We don't think of it until we lose it. I've been hospitalized twice with angina. And, oh, when they put that thing over my face and gave me oxygen and I could breathe again! . . . I just couldn't be too thankful."

"I had this girl friend who used to say, 'Thank you, God' for everything. We'd drive into the city and every time the light was green she'd say, 'Thank you.' One time she asked me, 'Did you notice that the last seven lights have been green?' She'd even say thank you for bad things. 'I don't like this,' she'd say, 'but thank you anyway. I believe it's for a reason. Help me see the reason.' "

Exercise 3: Letters to God (10 minutes)

Allow time for group members to read aloud from Exercise 7 in their workbooks and letters, poems, prayers or psalms they have addressed to the "Giver of Grace."

Exercise 4: Welcoming Grace (25 minutes)

Put on newsprint these words:

> *Whatever your mind can conceive,*
> *and your heart believe,*
> *you can achieve.*

Have participants sit comfortably with both feet on the ground and nothing in their laps. Have them shut their eyes and breathe slowly and deeply a few times. Explain that for a few minutes you are going to give them the opportunity to envision themselves fully open to Grace. Encourage them to relax and, being receptive, let images come on the screen of their minds' eyes of what they would be like if they were in the presence of total love and acceptance, loved for who they are and for who they are becoming.

How would you look? What would your posture be? The expression on your face? How would you feel? What would you be doing with your life? How would you be spending your money . . . your time? What interest would you be developing? What would your relationships be like? (Ask these questions slowly, deliberately, pausing sufficiently between them to allow the visioning to take place.)

When sufficient time has elapsed, invite them to open their eyes and use colored crayons to create a symbol, or image, of what they envisioned. When all have finished, have them display their symbols by attaching them with masking tape to their chests, and move into the final exercise.

A Time of Leave Taking (10 minutes)

The time has come to bring this series of twelve sessions to a close. The most appropriate way to part, perhaps, would be to mill around the room, allowing group members to speak freely and personally with whomever they wish.

When the time has finally come to conclude, we suggest that you form a circle once more. Some in the group may wish to say something to the entire group. Allow for that briefly, then we suggest that you sing together "Amazing Grace." The words are found on page 235 of *The Road Less Traveled*.

(We like to recall the fact that John Newton, who wrote the hymn, was captain of a slave ship until he repented of his sinful way of life and experienced the miracle of forgiveness.)

186